GOLF SCHOOL

DOUBLEDAY

NEW YORK   LONDON   TORONTO
SYDNEY   AUCKLAND

GOLF SCHOOL

The Tuition-Free

Tee-to-Green Curriculum

from Golf's Finest

High-End Academy

Jim McLean

PUBLISHED BY DOUBLEDAY

a division of Random House, Inc.

1540 Broadway, New York, New York 10036

DOUBLEDAY and the portrayal of an anchor with a dolphin are
trademarks of Doubleday, a division of Random House, Inc.

BOOK DESIGN BY DEBORAH KERNER

ILLUSTRATION BY RICHARD WAXBERG

Library of Congress Cataloging-in-Publication Data

McLean, Jim.
    Golf school: the tuition-free tee-to-green curriculum from golf's
finest high-end academy / Jim McLean. — 1st ed.
        p.   cm.
    1. Golf—Study and teaching.   I. Title.
GV962.5.M35   1999
796.352′07—dc21   98-52979
                                                        CIP

ISBN 0-385-49287-1

Printed in the United States of America

July 1999

First Edition

10 9 8 7 6 5 4 3 2 1

To my sons Matt and Jon,

who I hope do the best they can

in whatever walk of life they choose

and that they also have a great family.

My wife Justine and I

have been blessed with

two great boys.

ACKNOWLEDGMENTS

I have to thank Larry Dennis, who compiled tons of my notes and then personally went through two golf schools, plus observed two others. Larry truly captured the essence of our schools. I hope together we have produced a book that is a true quality work.

Thanks must go to my staff of master teaching professionals, who strive every day to make our instruction programs the best in the world. That means a total commitment to, as Tom Peters would say, towering competence. Our superstations house incredible technology, but it's the professionals using these tools that make all the difference.

My operational staff led by Warren Rogan, Kara Watter, and John O'Neill do a fantastic job working with the hotels, sending letters, and one hundred other small details that make a golf school successful. They have a major responsibility in making our guests feel special and in having all the behind-the-scenes activities run seamlessly.

Finally a special thank-you to all of our students who return to our schools year after year and give their personal recommendations, which are truly the lifeblood of our business.

CONTENTS

GOLF SCHOOL

I N T R O D U C T I O N

The reason you bought this book—or are even looking at it—is that you're a golfer, or you want to become a golfer, and you want to get better at playing the game.

Golf is an infinitely complex game, full of pleasures and rich rewards at every level but difficult, if not impossible, to learn without expert help. In a perfect world, each of us would have a skilled personal instructor who would help us develop a concept of swinging and playing and who would regularly coach us through the physical and mental drills, both off course and on, that would help us learn and improve. The tour professionals, the best players in the world, now all have coaches with whom they work on a regular basis. Unfortunately, that kind of help is not available to most amateur players, usually because they do not have the time, the money, or the access to quality instructors.

Given that, the next-best approach would be to attend a Jim McLean Golf School. There a student receives personal and personalized instruction in all aspects of the game from a cadre of Master Instructors who are the best in their field. They take each student through a comprehensive curriculum that covers exercises that will help him or her play better, swing mechanics, instruction on playing different shots, the correct mental approach, and on-course strategy and game management. The schools last from one to six days and offer a variety of specialized subjects, ranging from schools that cover the game in general to those that concentrate on areas like power, the short game, scoring, and playing. At any of these schools, students are given an evaluation of their current skills and then provided the tools to improve them.

With a very low student–teacher ratio and the use of video and the latest in computer technology, the golf schools offer an ideal learning situation. Students leave the school sometimes without their problems solved but always with their problems identified and the means to cure them. The rest, as in any endeavor, is up to the individuals and their willingness to put in the time and effort to develop their game to its highest potential.

The problem is that all top golf schools, quite frankly, are expensive, especially when you factor in travel, lodging, and meal costs. They also require students to carve out a specified period of time.

Fear not. If any of this is a problem for you, this book is the answer. Between these two covers you will be given all the instruction you would receive in all of McLean's schools. And it costs you only the price of the book. You will be taken on a step-by-step journey through a school, just as if you were on site. You will receive the same variety of instruction from McLean and his instructors that you would get at the school. And you will receive the same instruction in the specialized schools that you would get if you attended them.

The beauty of it is that you can learn at your own convenience at your home course, in your back yard, or in your living room. You can take your time in studying the text, the instructional drawings, and the photographs. And you can visit the school every day for as long as you like.

When you finish the book, you will have a clear vision of what our students have when they leave a Jim McLean Golf School. You will have the tools to improve your swing and your ability to play the game better. There is no one secret to playing golf well, no magic panacea. As with any activity you want to do well, playing good golf requires a measure of devotion, time, and effort. You might call it work, except that golf is a game, and even working at it can be fun. And after you have read and studied this book and applied the lessons contained in it, you will have a gigantic head start in playing this game to your potential.

What and How You Will Learn

Before beginning to read and work on the actual instruction in this book, it's important for you to understand what golf is and what it isn't.

Golf is a game in which you use no more than fourteen clubs to send a small ball into a cup at different distances, over all kinds of obstacles, in the fewest number of swings.

Golf is not an accumulation of tips, and the ability to play it well is not based on helter-skelter thoughts that usually have no bearing on each other. Unfortunately, that's the way a lot of golfers try to find improvement. A tremendous amount of information is out there now through the Internet, the Golf Channel, all the televised instruction shows, the golf magazines, and even tips in newspapers. That's not to mention the advice from your buddies in your Saturday foursome. Every golfer, you know, is a teacher. And since most amateurs really don't have any clear concept of the golf swing, most also don't even know what they are actually doing or trying to do. As a result, they tend to listen to anybody who is walking up and down the range offering advice. None of this bodes very well for somebody trying to improve his or her game. I always say, "Too much information can be worse than no information at all."

Golf is a game of fundamentals, of basic positions and motions that you must learn before you have a chance to play the game well. These fundamentals essentially apply to your grip, your body motion, and the club, and a wide range of subtopics apply.

It is my job in this book, just as it is in our schools, to make the golf swing—all of the different swings you use in golf—as simple as possible and to make your thoughts and concepts clear. This book can't make you a great player, but it can teach you to learn to play better golf. It can help you learn the fundamentals of golf and how to maximize the assets you possess. In other words, you may not have the physical skills or body structure of Tiger Woods or Ernie Els or Annika Sorenstam, but you can learn to play as well as your own talent and body will allow.

So always keep in mind that I can't teach you, and this book can't teach you, everything it takes to get better. Neither can a session in our schools. Your improvement depends for the most part on you and how hard you're willing to work to improve. This book provides the guidelines, the knowledge that will help you do that. It's up to you to put that knowledge to its best purpose. If you're willing to accept that responsibility, this book will help you become your own best teacher.

The Four Ways to Learn

In my system of teaching, I use a four-pronged process for learning golf, which I believe is the same for any sport. The first step is through verbal communication. Your instructor tells you what to do, or in this case you read the words in the book. The second is through visual demonstration, in this case through the pictures in the book. Or watch the really good players at your club or course. Or go to a PGA Tour or Senior PGA Tour or LPGA tournament and watch how the top players in the world swing. Their swings will vary, but if you look closely, you'll see that all their fundamentals are basically sound and they end up in startlingly similar positions in the critical area of the swing, the impact zone. This learning modality is a simple matter of "monkey see, monkey do." Children, for example, often learn best by copying. They don't need a detailed explanation of what to do. They just see a motion, copy it in their minds, and do it.

The third way to learn is kinesthetic, or feeling what your body is doing throughout the motion you are making or are trying to learn. To me and my instruction staff, this is the most important factor in learning to play golf well. Whether you are stroking a three-foot putt, playing a soft pitch, or hitting a full drive, you must ingrain a feel for the motion you need. Some call it "muscle memory," although it's really an image or sensation in the brain that enables you to re-create a swing consistently without having to think about the mechanics involved. That lets you focus on your target and the shot you want to play. To own a swing change you must actually be able to execute the new move. Understanding what to do does not mean you can perform the move. Our instructors must see it. You must feel it a new way and you must actually make the change. Often the instructor will glide the club to help you ingrain the new feel.

And the fourth way is through drills. Drills are great because they isolate small segments of your swing that need improvement. Also, once you learn the drill, you don't need the teacher. I'm a big believer in drills and I know how much they can help golfers. This book will provide some of the best drills we use on a daily basis at the schools.

Unfortunately, most golfers who have played for any length of time without good instruction have learned the wrong swing. That means that not only do you have to learn a new swing, you first have to unlearn the old one. At a very high level, Tom Kite is a classic example. Tom grew up with a backswing that he took too far to the inside and then too far inside to outside on the forward swing. The result was a low, swinging hook that ran a long way and worked well on Texas hardpan. But as soon as Tom played in his first professional tournament at Westchester Country Club, an old-line course in New York, he realized that his method was not going to work on the PGA Tour, where courses often require high shots into elevated greens. So he began working with Bob Toski on changing his swing to get that higher ball flight. That violates the old theory that says, "If you don't have it when you come out here, you're not going to find it here." Probably only someone with Kite's determination could have pulled it off.

That was in 1972, and as far as I know, Kite is still working on swing changes. I worked a lot with Tom over the last several years, especially in 1992, 1993, and 1994. In 1992 he won the U.S. Open with a swing in which he felt he was taking the club back straight to the outside, virtually lifting or elevating the clubhead vertically. Then he swung down feeling like he was trying to hit his left leg on his follow-through. The question is, did his swing really look like that? Of course not. The point is, that was the feel he was trying to ingrain to get further away from that early, flat, inside-out swing. That's why change is so difficult. You often have to exaggerate a motion, or feel that you are exaggerating it, to do it correctly. To move an inch, you might have to feel like you are going a mile. As Ken Venturi, the former U.S. Open champion and renowned golf analyst for CBS television, always told me, "When you make a change, it will most likely feel bad. That's good! If it feels good, you probably haven't changed a thing."

We make changes and we learn the golf swing in different ways, although often a drill works best. Remember, a drill is effective because it isolates a small area in your swing. This book is loaded with drills that will help both your full swing and your short game, and I encourage you to use them. It's easy to go to the practice tee and just beat balls, but that's usually counterproductive. More often than not, you're just ingraining bad habits. Working with drills may not seem to be as much fun, but believe me, you'll develop a better golf swing much more quickly. That's when you'll really start to have fun.

A System for the Individual Golfer

Our philosophy, in our schools and in this book, is that we don't teach a strict method. However, I do have a system and a strict method of *how* we teach. My system is unique in that I leave a lot of room for individual differences and allow my teachers to use all their creativity. We don't believe, as some other schools and instructors do, that everybody is going to fit into the same golf swing. Everybody is built differently, so there are a lot of different ways to make a golf swing and play golf and do it well. But we keep in mind basic fundamentals: body motion and club action. In our teaching method, you can do it your own way as long as you stay within the parameters or limits where we find good players who have been able to do it very well. I call those parameters the "corridors of success." This is a huge part of our teaching success. Once outside those corridors, virtually nobody in the history of the game has succeeded. I recommend an immediate change for super poor body positioning or an off-plane downswing.

In that sense, then, we do have a system of teaching, and you could fairly classify me as a system teacher. I worked a lot with Ken Venturi over the years, and probably the most important thing I learned from him was consistency. In other words, if you go to one of our teachers, you're going to get the same fundamentals, the same concepts, year in and year out. I believe our system offers the most solid foundation there is. It is based on fundamentals, yet we allow those individual corridors to success. The way we break down and analyze the swing is different from the way most instructors do it. We look for specific things. We look at fundamental positioning of the body and fundamental positioning of the club. We also look for the "death moves," actions or positions that are so far outside the corridors that they will cause you to hit poor shots forever. These are the faults we change right away in our students.

I believe that all top coaches in all other sports have a system. In golf, most of the well-known golf coaches say they don't. They're afraid to be called method teachers. Often these same instructors teach specific locations in the golf swing and you have to swing in an exact model action. To me, that is very restrictive teaching. However, having a method or a certain way of teaching does lend clarity to your message. It provides consistency to what you are telling students. Even if it doesn't fit everybody, the students who come back are going to receive the same message. To me, that's a whole lot better than having teachers who are in the search mode themselves. One month it's one concept and the next month another. That's very confusing and leads to a total loss of confidence in your students. I've seen many method teachers become very, very successful and really help people. Restrictive method teachers can't help the vast majority of golfers, but some golfers can get valuable information.

Jimmy Ballard is definitely a method teacher, and he was extremely popular through the '70s and early '80s. He had many top Tour players going to see him, and his schools drew extremely well. He's still very popular today, and that's a long span of time. By the way, I learned a lot of great things from Jimmy myself. He had a certain message that many golfers liked. I see that same thing in Ken Venturi, who has a certain idea of how the golf swing should be made, or Jackie Burke, Bob Toski, or the late Gardner Dickinson and Claude Harmon.

I've seen a lot of other teachers who changed their messages every few years or maybe more. I'm always worried about going to a teacher who tells you one thing one year, and when you go back the next year he says, "Oh, you know what, we're not doing that anymore. Now we're doing something else." That's terrible instruction.

I've come up with a system that leaves room for individuality, and I'm very comfortable with it. I've taught it since 1985. We don't change. Our schools operate in a consistent pattern, but within the parameters I've outlined we judge each individual separately and give him or her the help that best fits and is most likely to lead to improvement. That's the way I'd encourage you to study this book. I've tried to make it easy for you to search out the information that will best help you with your individual problems.

That said, there are a number of things we recommend and teach that will help everybody at any level, from the beginner to the Tour player. The first is a series of stretching drills that are specific to golf and will prepare your body for practice or play. Jason Jenkins, who is a Master Instructor on our staff, is also a kinesiologist and has helped devise some nice warm-up exercises.

Another is something that we pioneered in the '80s, when I first started doing schools. We began having our students do body drills without a club, folding their arms across their chests and coiling and uncoiling to increase their awareness of what the body should be doing in the swing. To my knowledge, that wasn't being done anywhere else at the time.

Setup, which is the way you stand to the ball, and alignment, which is how you aim the club and your body before the shot, are pretty much standard for every good player. There may be some variations to accommodate differences in body structure and shot tendencies—whether you want to fade the ball from left to right or draw it from right to left—but every good shot stems from a setup and an alignment that are basically the same, no matter what your particular swing might be. I call this the "universal fundamental"—setup, because even most teachers could agree on a proper setup.

The correct grip pressure is critical to a smooth and effective swing. I'll discuss this in detail later in the book. So is a relative absence of tension in the body at address and throughout the swing. Usually these two factors are interrelated, and they apply to all players, no matter their individual swing tendencies.

All of these factors are dealt with in the pages that follow.

The 25 Percent Theory

The cornerstone and centerpiece of our schools and this book, and a unique part of the Jim McLean system, is the 25 percent theory. As I worked during the winter of 1976–77 with Ken Venturi and went through the Tour Qualifying School (missing in the finals at Pinehurst), I began to look at golf in a different way, mainly in trying to identify how I missed qualifying. It seemed to me that the game could be divided into four key and equal parts, which are

- **the long game**
- **the short game**
- **the course management game**
- **the mental/emotional game.**

To my way of thinking, the management game and the mental game were just as important as the long game and the short game, once a player was reasonably proficient in those physical areas.

At that time I had been teaching for six months at Westchester Country Club in Rye, New York, a suburb of New York City. In the off-season I was playing the Florida winter tour and minitour events. Being a part-time teacher and part-time player gave me an excellent opportunity to test the theory I was developing.

I knew that for an advanced tournament player, the mental game was by far the most important element of the four. I knew from teaching that hitting the golf ball was the most important aspect of golf for the beginner. We all know that the short game lowers our scores more than anything else. And I had seen during my lifetime in golf that some players managed the golf course and their personal strengths and weaknesses much better than others. Often a less gifted player can shoot low scores by being mentally tough, mentally alert, and making no management mistakes.

Further exploration—talking with other professionals and examining how I really helped my students improve—validated the theory, and this concept became the centerpiece of my teaching system.

I'm sure I was the first teacher to talk about this and document it in books. In the early '80s I began speaking on teaching in the metropolitan PGA section and later began to do so nationally. I usually led off my remarks with the 25 percent theory, and I received a very positive response.

To a professional audience, I explained the theory this way. Take any two areas at which you want to be great. Which would you choose? Would that make you a tour player? Then I would argue that two was not enough. If you were not very good at any two of these areas, you couldn't play tournament golf.

For example, let's say you were a terrific ball-striker on the range and a great putter on the practice green. But if you had a bad mental game—you got very nervous and couldn't focus on the course—and a poor management game—you played low-percentage shots, didn't have a preshot routine, and didn't visualize or plan your shots—you had no chance to make it on the Tour. You just couldn't shoot low enough scores.

To be a Tour-caliber player, you need to be very good in at least three out of four of these areas. The great players are great in all four areas.

The long game, of course, encompasses your ball-striking, the full swing. This is the area in which most golfers spend most of their time and where they want to take instruction. They believe that if they can build a perfect golf swing, they can play perfect golf. This is folly. Nobody has ever done that, and even if you could, you still have the three other areas of golf to master. The long game is critically important, of course, and also the most fun to work at, but I encourage you to look carefully at the other three parts of the game.

We define the short game area as from 75 yards in for mid- and high handicappers, and from 100 yards in for better players. This includes putting, chipping, pitching, bunker play, and getting it up and down from trouble within that range. Since the best players in the game don't even hit 70 percent of the greens in regulation, you can see how important the short game is. If it's possible for you, the golf course is a great place to practice your short game.

The management game is simply having the knowledge and the discipline to manage yourself. That means preparing yourself in every way possible in order to reach your goals. This might include a fitness program, better diet, and perhaps just slowing down getting to the golf course. It also means managing your game around the course, to avoid trouble and take the safe route, to avoid unwise gambles unless the circumstances of your match or the tournament absolutely force you to take them, to focus on hitting the green rather than firing at dangerous hole locations, to use a preshot routine effectively. In other words, to play golf intelligently rather than foolishly.

The mental/emotional game and how you handle it determines your ability to take your range game to the golf course. Developing firm control of your mind and your emotions helps you play within yourself, frees your mind of extraneous thoughts and doubts, lets you concentrate on playing the game, and helps you perform more consistently to the level of your talent, especially in pressure situations.

Improvement in these last two areas, by the way, might reduce your scores more than any improvement you can make in the physical areas.

All four areas are covered thoroughly in our schools and in this book. This book gives you help in strengthening the areas in which you are weak. It will help you improve your swing and your ball-striking, and it will help you take that range swing onto the golf course and make it work there as well.

In every single lesson we give, our instructors must first listen and watch as you swing and describe your game. We must take in a lot of information quickly and size you up carefully. What part of your game is lacking? Of the four main areas of golf, where should we start? Many times it is not the long game, as most people would expect. Yet in a golf school, we get to cover important aspects of all four parts. I call that *total game teaching*.

Three Steps to Improvement

The Jim McLean system we use in our schools really boils down to a pretty simple three-step plan I've developed for getting better. Every instructor goes through this simple process with every student as we make necessary changes. Those steps are (1) What am I doing now? Today, on this date, what exactly am I doing? Not what I hope I'm doing, not what I think I'm doing, not what I was doing last year, but what I'm actually doing at the moment. (2) What should I do instead? If a Supreme Being appeared and granted me any golf swing I wanted, could I demonstrate it or even explain it? Probably not. Even if I knew my flaws, what should I do to correct the flaws I have and improve to the point where I have a swing that works effectively? (3) Finally, how do I make the change? Here is where our instructors and this book come in. In it are the concepts that will help you make the necessary changes.

Of course, that requires a very clear understanding of your golf swing and your areas of strength and weakness. Most amateurs don't have that understanding, simply because they've never taken time to analyze carefully what they do right or wrong, or because they don't know what in the swing causes good or bad results. Ideally, use a good camcorder and a VCR so you can tape your swing, and use the information in this book to critique it. Remember, there are three other areas of the game for your self-critique as well. In our schools, we use sophisticated video and a proprietary computer system to determine your swing faults. You can't take advantage of that, but you can take your own video and compare it to the positions you see in the photographs in this book. And you definitely should sit down for an hour or so and honestly assess how you play golf. Ask yourself some hard questions, and be brutally honest with the answers. Here's a sample list from our school questionnaire:

- **What is your best score in the last year?**
- **What is your best score ever?**
- **What is your current handicap?**
- **What is the lowest your handicap has ever been?**
- **How often do you play?**
- **Do you warm up and hit practice balls before you play?**

- How often do you practice?

- What is the average length of your practice sessions?

- What percentage of your practice time is given to the long game and to the short game?

- Are you a good driver? How many fairways do you hit per round? How far do you carry your tee shots with a driver? What is your average driving distance, carry and roll, under normal circumstances? (Be honest with this one, because it's critical. If you're not sure, go out on a fairway late some evening, hit several balls, and step them off.) Do you hit the ball high (too high?) or low (too low?)?

- Have you always been a good driver—or a bad driver?

- What type of driver do you use? Is the loft and the weighting correct for your typical ball flight?

- What are your normal shot tendencies? Do you fade the ball slightly from left to right? Do you slice it badly? Do you push the ball to the right? Do you draw the ball slightly from right to left? Do you hook it? Do you pull it to the left? Is your normal shot a combination of any of these? What is your bad-shot tendency?

- How is your iron play? How many greens do you hit in regulation each round? If that number is low, is it because bad driving leaves you in a poor position, or is it because of poor iron shots?

- How good or bad is your short game from off the green? From a reasonable distance around the green, how many times do you get up and down in two, out of how many chances, during the course of a round? Do you have trouble pitching the ball? Are your chip shots finishing too far from the hole? What percentage of your bunker shots do you get out and on the green on the first try? What percentage of the time do you get up and down in two? What is your biggest problem in the bunker, skulling it over the green or hitting the shot fat and leaving it in the sand?

- How good a putter are you really? How many three-putts do you average each round? Do your long putts tend to wind up long or short? What percentage of your three- and four-foot putts do you make? Do you tend to miss your putts to the right or to the left? Do you have trouble reading greens—are you often surprised when the putt breaks less or more than you anticipated?

- How good is your course management? In retrospect, how many strokes do you waste with ill-advised shot selections? How many strokes do you waste by taking low-percentage gambles instead of playing the high-percentage safe shot? How many times a round do you play a shot that you haven't practiced or are not particularly skilled at, rather than a safer shot that you know you can make and that will put you in a decent position for your next shot?

- How does your on-course ball-striking compare with that on the practice tee?

- Are you able to relax on the golf course, or are you extremely nervous?

- What techniques do you use to relax?

- Do you visualize your shots?

- Do you have an image of your golf swing?

- How mentally tough are you? How do you handle pressure situations? Does self-doubt creep in? Do you become overly nervous under pressure? Do you let your mind wander to the consequences rather than focusing on executing the shot at hand?

- Do you have any physical limitations or injuries?
- Are you right- or left-handed?

These are the basic questions you need to ask yourself. Many others will help you further analyze your swing and playing tendencies. Armed with honest answers, you then can find information in this book that will help you work on and improve your most serious problems.

How to Practice and Improve

One of the major advantages in our golf schools is that we don't have a set program for each group or each school that we conduct. That's a major departure from all other golf schools I've observed. We don't know what handicap grouping we'll have in any particular school, nor do we know what students' specific needs will be. So rather than establishing a regimented daily schedule for all, we set up our schools so we can adjust to the students in each particular one and deal with their needs. Some students may want more help with the driver. Some may need more help with the short game. Some may need to spend more time in the practice bunker or on the putting green. So we'll have instructors in these different areas to provide that extra instruction and practice.

I got the idea from football—Bruce Coslet, then head coach of the New York Jets and now the head coach of the Cincinnati Bengals, and Jim Young, then head coach at Army. Bruce played for Paul Brown and coached with Bill Walsh, among others. Plus I've read a ton of books about other great coaches, like John Wooden, Bobby Knight, Bill Walsh, and Rick Pitino. In visiting their training camps, I saw that they didn't have the whole team working on the same things at the same time. They would split the team into groups—the receivers and quarterbacks in one part of the field, the defensive linemen in another, and so forth, all working on their specialties. I figured that sort of system would work in golf schools, and it does. It also can work for you as you conduct your own school. Once you've determined your specific area or areas of need, you can spend the majority of your time working in that area. Identify exactly what you need to be working on in your game.

Of course, just as a football team eventually has to come together and work as a unit, so you eventually have to deal with the whole golf swing and the whole game. You may work on your swing in parts, but in the end you have to mold those parts into a whole. Then you have to take all the elements of the game, from driving to putting, sound preshot routine technique, and management skills, and go out on the course and play with them effectively.

Improvement comes much faster with intelligent practice. Always go to the practice tee with a firm intention and a plan of action. Remember, making a swing change and hitting perfect shots are two different things. By that I mean that when you are making a swing change, you must forget ball-flight results for a while. Otherwise, you slip back into old mistakes just for the sake of slightly better immediate results. This is simply human nature. It's also a prime reason I use nets or have students make a lot of swings without a ball. However, you must come to terms with this simple truth: a significant swing change is not always easy. In fact, it usually takes hard work and, of course, time. Our best students accept this, and they are the ones who make the most progress and who dramatically improve their ball-striking skills. Evaluate yourself and your shots intelligently.

Making a game plan for your practice time (and your playing time, for that matter) is important. That in itself requires discipline. You must be realistic. As I've discussed, determine what you need to work on most in each area of the game, then decide how much time you will devote to each of those areas. Stick to that plan. The act of writing out such a plan is as important as anything else you will do to improve. I also recommend that you make notes during and after each practice session, keeping track of what works and what doesn't and writing down how you feel as you make the changes.

As you practice and make changes in your swing from the information you will get in this book, it's important to keep a few points in mind. When you are developing new skills, it's imperative to conceptualize the new moves clearly. You must grasp the fundamentals, and the fundamentals I give you in this book may surprise you. Often golfers are not really aware of what a golf fundamental is and is not. As soon as you have achieved such mastery, you can apply that knowledge. In the beginning, you will be laying the foundation on which you are going to build the best swing you can make.

Repetition is the key to learning new habits and unlearning old ones. You can't do either with a half-dozen swings. Your drills and your new swing thoughts must be repeated on a regular basis, in practice swings, practice drills, and actually hitting shots, over a considerable period of time. Practice the applicable drills until you achieve the results you want. You strengthen swing fundamentals by precisely practicing drills tailored to correct your swing faults. This is the fastest path to meaningful change. Again, that doesn't mean it will be as fast as you probably want it. It takes time for the muscles to accept what you are telling them to do. Your old swing won't disappear in half an hour, especially when it took you years to develop it. So be patient. Allow plenty of time for your new technique to develop. And remember that you probably will regress before you progress.

Often a new move will cause some discomfort and confusion. Suffer the discomfort until it is no longer uncomfortable. By perseverance, you will find comfort in the new habit. Confusion often means you are beginning to understand something in a new way—and I always look at this in a positive fashion.

Remember, it is the quality of practice that counts, not the quantity of balls you hit. Try to practice where you can concentrate without being disturbed. As I learned from great coaches in other sports, a short, focused practice session is a great way to maximize your practice time. Spend a lot of time doing your drills. Then practice your swing, but at first you may have to forget ball-flight results. Make good use of your practice swings without a ball. Don't make them randomly—keep in mind what you're working on and make them real swings. When you get tired, stop hitting shots. Or go off and practice your putting or chipping, then return to full-swing practice when you are refreshed.

If it's possible, practicing by yourself on the course is an excellent idea. Hit several shots from different situations, always working on your new swing keys.

Even after you've hit some good shots using your new concepts, as you certainly will, keep your expectations realistic. Be aware that your new swing probably won't work as well on the course, at least at first, as it did on the practice tee. Extra-high expectations tend to add pressure, and you don't need that in a learning situation.

Speaking of expectations, I've found it most helpful to keep a student's expectations at a very realistic level. I want our students to outperform my expectations for them, not the opposite. That's a little teaching technique that has really worked tremendously for me over many, many years. Try it yourself.

If you must play while you are making a swing change (and you probably will), don't worry about your score and don't play for too much money with your friends. Remember, under pressure you may return to the old, comfortable swing, especially if you don't get immediate results from the new swing thoughts. Take it from me, hang in there. Give your new method a fair chance. Trust what you are trying to do to improve, even if it takes a while to get there. I find it sad that many golfers keep obvious mistakes in their swings for ten, twenty, or more years and continue to be disappointed in their golf year after year. They won't accept a short period of discomfort that could eventually change their game and allow them to succeed. Remember, garbage in, garbage out.

Always remember, as you strive to get better, that there is no magic move. There is no magic bullet or magic pill that you can take to make you better without paying the dues. We hear and read about these new, magical concepts all the time—some revolutionary new way of swinging the club, a different way of gripping it, and so forth. They are nonsense. The way to get better is to rely on the proven fundamentals, develop a game plan for improvement, and be patient.

This also applies to mental magic pills—"If you think this way, you will play much better." Well, I've learned a lot from all the sports psychologists I've had the opportunity to work with, and I can tell you that there is also no magic way to think. I've worked extensively with the best mental trainers in America. Developing the right mental approach to practice and playing is a long process. Actually, the things that sports psychologists work on for the most part are commonsense ideas—visualize your shots, have confidence when you play them, focus, don't try too hard, be mentally tough. Most good players know all that, but it takes a long time to mold everything into a consistent and effective mental approach.

In the end, the mental magic comes mainly from your willingness and ability to develop your complete game. I'm reminded of the story about the late Claude Harmon, who was talking one day with his sons, all of whom are well-known golf professionals. The boys were discussing how important sports psychologists had become and mentioned that Claude had never talked to them that much about the mental part of the game.

Claude listened for a quite a while and finally said, "Hey, guys, wait a minute here. Whatever happened to a square clubface at impact?"

One of his sons said, "Well, I'm not sure, Dad. I think it's still important."

"Well, damn, I guess it is important," Claude barked. "Ben Hogan had a square clubface at impact. He hit bullets straight down the fairway every time. You think you're going to have confidence when you look up and that ball is going straight every time? Damn right you will! If you can hit it great, if you can really play, you'll have confidence."

I've had a quote from Bobby Knight, the legendary Indiana basketball coach, on my wall for many years. He said, "Confidence is bullshit. Either you can play or you can't." When I later met Coach Knight and spent some great time with him, I discussed this old quote. He really got fired up and explained his thoughts even more dramatically.

What he said was that when you have the fundamentals and the mechanics, when you can really hit the shots, your confidence is going to soar. When you've done the work, when you've done the drills, you'll be able to play. I'm pretty much in that camp. If you've done the work, if you've paid the price, if you've been out there working at it, hitting the balls, getting good teaching, then you know what you are supposed to do and when you can execute. You're going to have a lot more confidence and you'll be a lot tougher mentally when the time comes to win a golf tournament or a two-dollar Nassau if you busted your butt to get there. You are certainly more likely to come through than somebody who sat in a room and visualized being good. We live in a society that wants and expects immediate results and an easy way out. Believe me, golf isn't like that. Improvement comes to different people at different speeds. But nobody gets really good at golf without serious effort.

I find that a humble, patient, and consistent approach to your practice leads to a very strong mental approach to the game and a much better chance of achieving success.

So that's what we're going to start working on right now.

Part One

THE
FULL-SWING
SCHOOL

The long game, the full swing, is the area in which most golfers are interested and where they spend the most time practicing. There's a simple reason for that—it's the most fun! Hitting the ball in the center of the clubface feels so solid that it's like cutting through butter. It is one of the great joys of golf. Hitting a long, blistering drive down the center of the fairway with a slight draw on it and seeing it smoke down the fairway is a tremendous thrill.

We all also know that the short game is extremely important, and I urge you to develop yours to the fullest. Scoring is, after all, what the game is all about, and nobody can score well without a good short game. I've seen lots of players who skank the ball around the golf course because they can't hit the center of the clubface, but since they're good chippers and putters, they can score respectably. But I'm not sure how much fun they're having. Hitting the ball solidly is fun!

Ben Hogan once said, "If you can't drive the ball, you can't play good golf." Byron Nelson said, "The most important club in the bag, in my opinion, is the driver."

Although that statement is controversial, I agree. Being able to drive the ball long and straight allows the golfer to play an aggressive game and to play offensive golf. Driving the ball poorly makes you a defensive player. It keeps you from playing the hole the way the architect designed it, and that's always the hardest way to play. Yes, you can scrape the ball around and make a decent score if you have a good short game, but that's more work than fun. It's also hard on the nerves, which may tend to give way late in the round in crucial situations.

So in my system we don't diminish the importance of the long game. I give it a full 25 percent of the total. It's what gets you started on every hole and gets you to the green the proper way. It makes great golf possible, and it has the tremendous added benefit of intimidation. You will always have a sense of power over your opponent when you can dominate him or her from tee to green.

The Modern Swing versus the Classic Swing

As I mentioned earlier, there are many ways to swing a golf club and hit the ball very well. I believe that as long as you stay within the corridors of success, you should be in good shape. A good example lies in the comparison of the so-called modern swing with the classic swing of earlier eras. It's a comparison that might be valuable for you to make as you assess your own swing tendencies and capabilities.

The classic swing, with more emphasis on footwork and hip turn, will always be a great and effective swing. It is defined by Bobby Jones and Sam Snead, among many others, and that's not bad company.

The modern swing is defined by more lower-body resistance on the backswing, less footwork, and a more restricted hip turn. It is an efficient swing that produces power and accuracy if you're able to accomplish it. Players like Tiger Woods, David Duval, Nick Price, and Ben Hogan (after he restructured his swing early in his career) represent this tighter swing action.

I've found that some amateurs do better with the old-style swing, focusing more on active footwork and a slightly bigger hip turn. Others are more effective with less footwork and a restricted hip turn. It depends on your body structure, your strength, and most of all your flexibility. If you're not very flexible, you'll probably need more hip turn and footwork to increase the length and speed of your swing. If you have adequate flexibility, you can make a big enough shoulder turn while restricting your feet and hips. That will be a major asset. But don't pick a model for your swing until you determine these factors.

We spend a lot of time in our schools on body drills, and you should do the same on the drills I give you in this book. My old friend David Glenz (the 1998 PGA Teacher of the Year), Mike Lopuszynski, and I pioneered extensive use of body drills when we did our first schools in the mid-1980s. They help you understand how the body works in the swing, and we have had great success teaching fundamental moves to students at our schools. The concept is simple—the swinging of the club and the movement of the body are coordinated. Most amateurs focus on their arms, their hands, and the club, but they don't really think much about how the body should work in the swing. The better and simpler your body motion is, the more powerful and repeatable it is. That makes the job that your hands and arms do much easier. Once you understand what you want to do with your swing, you can either increase footwork, hip turn, shoulder turn, and head rotation, or you can reduce them. You can emphasize your body movement and coordinate the swinging of the club, or you can focus on swinging the hands, arms, and club and coordinate the movement of the body to that. The result can be the same. How you go about it depends on your individual assets and liabilities.

Dispelling the Myths

To illustrate further that there is more than one way to swing a golf club effectively, let me discuss a few myths that have grown up in the cult of golf instruction . . . and tell you why, along with giving some examples, they are indeed myths.

MYTH NO. 1:

There is a perfect grip.

- Players with strong grips (turned to the right): Paul Azinger, Billy Casper, Fred Couples, Bernhard Langer, Bruce Lietzke, Lee Trevino, David Duval
- Players with weak grips (turned to the left): Johnny Miller, Corey Pavin, Bill Rogers, Curtis Strange, Jose Maria Olazabal
- Players with unusual grips: Bob Estes, Andy Bean, Ed Fiori, Claude Harmon, Henry Picard, Judy Rankin, Gene Sarazen, Lanny Wadkins
- Players with interlocking grips: Tom Kite, Jack Nicklaus, Bruce Lietzke, Tiger Woods, Nancy Lopez

REALITY:

There are many great players holding the club in different ways. There is no perfect grip. It is always good to have an excellent grip; however, slight adjustments can be made to change ball flight or influence swing path. The grip, in the end, is simply a connection of the golfer to the golf club. If that golfer can return the clubface squarely to the golf ball with speed and consistency, he has found the perfect grip for himself.

MYTH NO. 2:

Point the club at the target at the top of the backswing.

- Players who lay the club off (pointing away from the target line): Doug Ford, Raymond Floyd, Ben Hogan, Peter Jacobsen
- Players who cross the line (pointing toward or across the target line): Gay Brewer, Jack Nicklaus, Calvin Peete

REALITY:

There is no perfect position at the top. Check out a professional tour. They are all different. Any teacher that tells you the clubshaft must be parallel to the target line at the top of the backswing with the clubface square hasn't studied golf swings.

MYTH NO. 3:

You must draw the ball from right to left to play effectively.

- Some players who fade the ball: Fred Couples, Jay Haas, Ben Hogan, Hale Irwin, Jack Nicklaus, Al Geiberger, Corey Pavin, Dan Pohl, Jeff Sluman, Craig Stadler, Lee Trevino, Ken Venturi

REALITY:

At the top level of golf, the fade is the ultimate control shot.

MYTH NO. 4:

Keep your head still during the swing.

- Your head has its own swing: The chin pivots to the right on the backswing, returns to the ball at impact, and releases to the target after impact. No great player has had a steady head. The head either swivels or moves side to side or does a little of both. What it does not do is stay still.
- Often the head and spine move laterally, back and forth.
- Keeping your head rigidly in place can produce the following negatives: a reverse pivot, hanging back, tension, back problems.

REALITY:

Keeping your head absolutely still can cause tension. As Harvey Penick said, "Show me a golfer who doesn't move his head and I'll show you a person that can't play golf."

MYTH NO. 5:

Golf is a left-sided game.

- Golf should be a two-sided game.
- Use *equal* grip pressure with both hands.
- Focus on the left or right side only if it produces good results. Many great players focus on the right side. I learned a lot of my golf instruction from Ken Venturi and Jimmy Ballard. Both were pure right-side teachers.

It's okay to focus on either the left side, the right side, or both sides together. Whatever works is fine with me.

As you can see from the list of players who vary from the so-called perfect, golf is an individual sport that can be played many different ways. Always remember, though, our teachers are trained to use the corridors of success, and you will learn much more about this as you read on.

All these variations work because each player has gained a feel for what makes his or her particular swing effective. So let me repeat something I wrote earlier, because it is worth repeating. A major part of golf ultimately becomes a feeling. Your swing is not just the sum of all the little parts that I'll give you. It is a feeling that you try to get into your muscles each day when you go out and start hitting balls, getting ready to play.

Whatever you might be working on changing—the grip, the setup, a particular part of your swing, or the full swing—don't worry if it feels awkward or funny. Actually, that's a good sign. That means you are doing something different, something that will lead to improvement. If you don't feel the change, and then don't execute the change, you don't own the change. By that I mean that knowing what to do and/or understanding what to do in no way means you can do it. Sure, it helps, but to own a change you must show me you can actually do it. Remember, I have to see it. Then that feeling must become ingrained, so that after a while it no longer feels awkward and will work for you on the golf course without your having to think about it.

Doing specific drills is a wonderful way for a new feeling to become ingrained. So is making practice swings and partial swings, if those swings are done properly. Spend a lot of time doing that. Just hitting a large number of golf balls doesn't necessarily make you better. In fact, it could make you worse, if you are consistently making the same incorrect movement over and over. You are simply training your muscles to do the wrong thing. Don't make the mistake of practicing bad habits. The longer you do that, the harder it will be to make the proper fundamental changes. When you see an older golfer who is frustrated with his game and who owns a terrible-looking golf swing, you're looking at someone who never paid the price. He hung in for a lifetime with a bad swing—and he will own it forever.

Preparing Your Body To Play

Golf could be one of the most difficult sports to play, requiring the most precision, which in turn requires hand-eye coordination and a body that responds the way you want it to. Yet I see an awful lot of amateurs who rush out of their cars and onto the first tee early in the morning without making any attempt to prepare their bodies properly to play.

You might be able to get away with that when you're eighteen and still supple. But as you grow older, and especially as you get more sedentary, your muscles stiffen, and it takes you a lot longer to warm them up so they can work at maximum efficiency.

We start each daily session at our schools with the series of warm-up exercises illustrated here, and I encourage you to do the same every time you go out to practice or play.

Start from the Ground Up

Here's a sentence you could almost take straight to the bank: the better your body motion is, the better a player you will be. You see some different-looking swings on the professional tours, and they all produce good shots. But if you mentally chop off the arms of those players and just look at what their bodies are doing, you'll see that the body motions are all very similar. There is a shift of the weight to the right leg (or left for a left-hander) as the upper body coils. Coming down, there is a shift of weight to the left side as the hips begin to turn and the upper body stays coiled. Then the upper body unwinds and you go to the finish with all the weight on their front side.

To do this well, you have to begin with the setup. You must be set up properly to the ball. Great golf is played from the ground up. All successful golf swings, and subsequent successful play on the course, start with good setup and alignment. The better you become, the more you'll find that swing problems usually start in these two areas. Consequently, that's where you'll find the solutions when your shots start to go bad. And that's why it's so important to get this part right as you try to improve your game. As Ken Venturi always hammered home to me, "Players don't lose their golf swings. Rather, they lose their position at setup." A key point we make at the school is that the shot is missed before you even draw the club away.

Set Up for Success

Let's look at your posture, how you set up to the ball. Again, there is room for individuality, but here's how to build a fundamentally sound stance to the ball. Ideally, go through this sequence in front of a mirror, at home or at your course. You should do it from a head-on position, looking directly into the mirror, and from the side views, looking at the target and looking away from the target. That way you can see what the feeling of a good setup looks like.

First, lay a club down between your feet, splitting your body in half. For a five-iron shot, spread your feet so the insides of your heels are just on the outsides of your hips. For a driver, you will want your stance a little wider. For the fairway woods, the stance is just slightly narrower than for the driver, and for the long irons it is just slightly narrower yet. As you move down into the shorter irons, it can be a little narrower than the five-iron stance. For all full shots, I like to see the legs pinned inward. That means braced and angled slightly from the feet to the hips.

Warm-up Drills *(above)* Hold the club above your head with arms extended as shown (1). Bend forward from the hips as far as you can, stretching the lower back and hamstring muscles, and hold for a few seconds (2). Hold the club above your head, bend to the left and hold (3), and to the right and hold (4) to stretch side muscles. (*Tony Roberts*)

1.

2.

1.

2.

32

3.

4.

3.

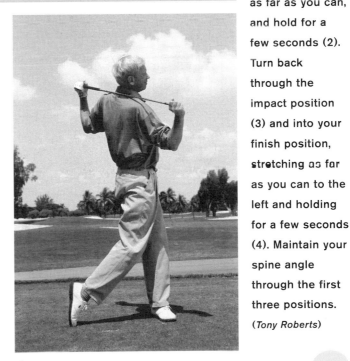

4.

Warm-up Drills (*below*) Assume your address position while holding the club across the back of your neck (1). Turn into your top-of-backswing position, turning as far as you can, and hold for a few seconds (2). Turn back through the impact position (3) and into your finish position, stretching as far as you can to the left and holding for a few seconds (4). Maintain your spine angle through the first three positions. (*Tony Roberts*)

1.

2.

Warm-up Drills

Assume your address
position with the club held
across your back and
between your elbows (1).
Turn as far as you can to the
right and hold (2). Turn back
to the left as far as you can
and hold (3). Feel the stretch
in both positions. (*Tony
Roberts*)

3.

Our system of teaching talks about two critical connections. The first is your hands to the golf club, and the second is your feet to the ground. Let's first discuss the feet to the ground. How your feet are placed on the ground affects how much your knees can turn and how much your hips can turn, which in turn affect how much your upper body turns. Set your right foot fairly straight or perpendicular to the target line. For older golfers or less supple individuals, turn the right toe out 15 degrees to 20 degrees, but don't point it out too much or there won't be anything for you to wind up against what we call the right-let post. There will be no resistance in the right leg. To gain hip-turn in the backswing, you should turn the right foot out a little extra so you can a little more turn on the backswing. But for normal purposes, the foot should be relatively close to perpendicular.

We want the left foot toed out more, about 25 or 30 degrees. Why? Because that makes it much easier to rotate through the shot and get your weight onto your left foot. It gives you a much freer range of motion in turning over your left hip or your left leg on your follow-through. Try setting your left foot perpendicular like your right and swing into a follow-through. Most golfers will feel like they get stuck. So turn the left foot out to achieve freedom of motion onto your left leg.

Once you have established your stance—your connection with the ground—the next step is to get into a good golf posture. To do this efficiently, use the following sequence. Stand erect, your legs straight, take your hands and put them against your hip joints, then force your hips back. Feel like your back hip pockets are going up as your upper body bends from the hips, yet keep your chest up, standing proud. Now add a little bit of knee flex. Let your knees bend slightly, just enough to relieve the tension in your straight legs. Feel that the weight is on the insides of your legs. I like to feel that my knees are pinched in a little and that my legs are angled in. Now let your shoulders relax and your arms drop so they are basically hanging (more on that later), and let your chin drop slightly (not so much that it droops against your chest). Don't slouch or round out the lower back. Keep your

The five-iron setup, face-on
(*Tony Roberts*)

The five-iron setup, down-line
(*Tony Roberts*)

The driver setup, face-on
(*Tony Roberts*)

The driver setup, down-line
(*Tony Roberts*)

spine straight to a point between your shoulder blades. Your upper shoulders will appear slightly rounded because they are relaxed, and the spine will curve or tilt at the top, up to the top of your head. This is very important and not often understood.

Because your right or trailing hand is lower on the club than your left or lead hand, your right shoulder will be slightly lower than your left, and your spine will tilt slightly to the right, away from the target. However, remember that these angles are small. Your spine will tilt only a few degrees away from the target. Always avoid large angles or tilts. That's a good rule.

Looking straight at the golfer, there can be an angle or break between your left forearm and the shaft of the club. I always want the grip end of your golf club to be aligned just inside the seam of your slacks. Anywhere between your body center and the seam is okay. That's the corridor. If you set your hands too high at address so that the shaft is pointing at, say, your chest, you'll be in a "decocked" position, which creates tension. You will also have trouble taking the club back on the correct plane and will hinder your wrist set. If your hands are lower and in the proper position, they are already some-what set, and it will be much easier to get into that right-angle L position in the middle of your backswing.

To keep your balance during the swing, your weight should be dis-tributed about fifty-fifty from right foot to left foot and also fifty-fifty between the balls of your feet and the heels. Move your feet, trying to feel a balanced position. Notice that Tour players and good amateurs keep their feet moving (some to a greater extent than others) as they set up to swing. They're simply trying to establish and feel a balanced position. If your weight is prop-erly distributed from front to back, a friend should not be able to push you over either forward or backward. One of the accepted adages in golf is that your weight should be on the balls of your feet and even somewhat toward the toes. I find that to be very dangerous, because too many people confuse balls of the feet with toes, and getting your weight too far forward is the worst mistake you can make. If you're going to make a mistake, toward the heels is better. But fifty-fifty between the balls and the heels is best.

At this point, you should feel as if you are in an athletic position and braced against the earth, like an infielder in baseball, a quarterback or a linebacker, a basketball player guarding an opponent, a tennis player awaiting serve, or just about any other athlete in any sport—you should feel balanced, your legs lively, ready to move in either direction, which indeed is what you have to do in a golf swing.

Practice getting into that proper setup position as often as you can. It's easy to do at home in front of your bedroom mirror, or almost anyplace else (it might look a little funny in an airplane aisle or on a downtown street, but that's up to you). Practice it until you can step into it comfortably and correctly without having to think about the individual adjustments. Then, when the feeling is ingrained, keep practicing so you don't lose it. Feelings that aren't reinforced can go away a lot faster than the time it takes to learn them. Remember, proper posture angles are crucial to making a good golf swing, and good balance at setup is a huge key in staying in balance throughout the swing.

Aiming the Club and the Body

That good setup you've just achieved won't do you much good if you don't aim correctly. You may hit some good shots at first, but they'll often be going in the wrong direction. And pretty soon you'll begin to make some adjustments instinctively during your swing to get the ball going toward your target, and pretty soon after that you will be totally lost. So aim your clubface and your body correctly to take advantage of good posture.

In our schools, we use a large clock (see illustration) painted on the ground to give a great visual image of both correct aim and alignment and

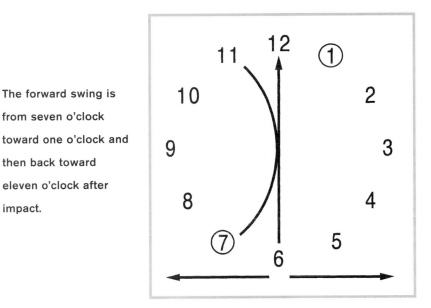

The forward swing is from seven o'clock toward one o'clock and then back toward eleven o'clock after impact.

the correct path and plane of the swing. Take a close look at the illustration and keep this image in your mind.

A line drawn from six to twelve o'clock represents your target line for a straight shot (forget the draws and fades for a moment; I'll get into that later). The target line is the most important line in golf for you as a player. Your club should be placed on that line, the face perpendicular to it and pointing at the target. Your feet, knees, hip, shoulders, and eyes all should be aligned parallel to the target line and perpendicular to your clubface for standard shots. In other words, you are set parallel left of the target line. Imagine railroad tracks. Your target line is the outside track on which you set your clubhead. Your feet are on the inside track. But remember, unlike real railroad tracks, which appear to narrow as they disappear in the distance, your imaginary tracks don't. That is, for a shot of, say, 180 yards, the outside track will run to the flag but the inside track will appear to be running perhaps to the left edge of the green. You should have the sensation that that's where your body is aligned, too.

Hold a club
across the top of
your shoulders
and check to see
that your
shoulders are
aligned parallel to
your target line.
(*Tony Roberts*)

Golf
School

Too many players align their bodies with the target, which means the clubface is actually aimed way to the right of the target. This is by far the most common setup alignment mistake we see at our schools. This mistake leads to other swing faults, such as taking the club away too far to the inside and/or coming over the top of the ball. So align parallel left—from this position you have the best chance of getting your swing on the correct plane and the ball started on line with minimum sidespin.

If there is any one thing I could give you with this book, it would be to relax your wrists, arms, and shoulders. "Tension kills the golf swing." I've probably said that line to 100,000 students. Set up as free of tension as possible. You'll have to have a certain amount of finger pressure, but too much tension ruins the swing. Check to see if the muscles in your hands, forearms, and shoulders are tensed. If so, back away, breathe deeply, exhale slowly, and shake out the tension. Then set up to the ball again in a relaxed fashion. On a scale of one to ten, I developed specifically to identify grip pressure, with light being one and supertight being ten, keep your grip pressure at about five or less. In the segment on the grip, I'll tell you how to determine that.

Ball Position Is Critical

Ball position—the place where you play the ball in relation to your feet and your swing center—is vital in making solid contact and producing shots that have the right trajectory, direction, and distance. I mention that here, but I'll go into more detail in the section "Why the Ball Travels the Way It Does."

The Grip

Your grip—the way you hold the club—is instrumental in controlling the motion of the club, especially the clubface. I've never felt that grip is the most important factor in a good golf swing, as some other teachers do; I've always believed that the motion of the body is more important. That's not to downplay the importance of a good grip. Your body and arms can't move the club correctly if you have a grip that won't let that happen.

I see a lot of good and great players with widely varying grips, but it's always advantageous to have a good grip. Let's look at how you build a basic grip, then discuss some of the variations.

In the left hand, the handle of the club lies diagonally across the palm, starting at the base of the forefinger and running up under the heel pad. It's important that the handle be held firmly between the heel pad and the last three fingers of the left hand to provide support throughout the swing. As you close your hand over the club, the thumb should lie slightly to the right side of the handle and the V formed by your thumb and forefinger should point somewhere between your chin and right shoulder. The so-called ideal is to see two knuckles of the left hand, but that's something we'll discuss in a moment.

The right-hand grip should be even more in the fingers. It's as if you were trying to hit a nail with a hammer. If you hold the hammer in your palm, you can barely cock it off the ground—your lever is restricted. If you hold it in your fingers, you can hinge it up and unhinge it easily as you strike

Building a Grip

The club lies diagonally across the left palm, from the base of the forefinger to under the heel pad (1). The left thumb lies slightly on the right side of the handle (2). The right-hand grip is more in the fingers (3), with the right thumb slightly on the left side of the handle and the forefinger crooked around the handle (4). The little finger of the right hand overlaps the forefinger of the left (5).

(*Tony Roberts*)

1.

2.

3.

4.

5.

the nail. It's the same with a golf shot. The right thumb should lie slightly to the left side of the handle. The right forefinger should be crooked around the handle and squeezed together with the thumb, as if you were shooting a pistol, and the V formed between the two should point in the same direction as that on the left hand. The left thumb should lie snugly between the two pads or cavity of the right hand. There should be no space anywhere between the two hands as they join together.

The little finger of the right hand overlaps the forefinger of the left or wraps around it. This is called the overlapping grip. But that too is far from an absolute. You can interlock that little finger with the forefinger of the left. As I indicated earlier, Jack Nicklaus does it, and that's not bad for starters. You can also use what is (erroneously) called the baseball or ten-finger grip, in which all the fingers and thumbs of both hands are on the handle of the club. Bob Rosburg and Jane Geddes used this grip, and both are major championship winners.

Let's look at knuckles showing the difference between a "weak" grip and a "strong" grip. If you look down at your completed grip and see that your hands are turned to the left or toward the target with just one knuckle showing, that's known as a weak grip. There was a time, back when I was in college, where all the good players were trying to use that type of grip. The theory was that it didn't allow as much rotation of the hands and forearms, so you could hit the ball straighter. It eliminated the hook. Well, unless you were very strong, you also couldn't hit it as far. Nowadays, a lot of the top players—David Duval and Fred Couples come immediately to mind—are playing with strong grips. They have three knuckles showing. Duval probably has all four knuckles showing. I can think of only one Tour player at the moment who has a weak grip, and that's Corey Pavin. And he's a guy who doesn't hit the ball very far. So if you are going to err, I'd prefer that you err on the strong side. As you get better, and if you get to hooking the ball too much, you can gradually weaken your grip, turning it more to the left.

Any change in your grip is difficult. But a good grip is an investment, so it's worth making a change to get it right. No good player ever forgets the importance of his or her grip for very long. He or she is always tinkering with it, because it does change over time, sometimes almost daily, and you have to keep checking it. Don't get complacent with it. I have worked with a number of the top LPGA players. For example, Liselotte Neumann and Jane Geddes have both won the U.S. Women's Open. The first time each came to see me, I changed her grip. I doubt if they ever would have done it on their own.

So get your grip right. Start out strong and adjust from there if you have to.

The pressure points in your grip are in the last three fingers of your left hand, the middle two fingers of the right, and the connection between the pocket or life lines of your right hand and your left thumb. I see way too many amateurs with their right thumbs too much on top of the shaft and applying pressure with that right thumb. That's a no-no, because it activates the top of the right forearm and tends to throw the club outward and downward on the downswing. The right thumb should just lie slightly to the side of the shaft, and you should not exert any pressure there. Applying pressure with the last three fingers of the left hand and the middle two of the right hand activates the bottom portions of the forearms, and that's what you want. Very important!

How much pressure you should have at those points may be even more critical than grip position. If you hold the club too lightly, you won't be able to control it properly throughout the swing. The swing exerts a lot of force, and with a too-light grip, the handle will tend to move around in your hand. However, that's rarely a problem we see at our schools. If you strangle the club, which many amateurs tend to do, you'll tighten the muscles in your arms and shoulders, which prevents you from making a full and correct swing. It simply will not flow and build speed.

I've devised a system for our schools that can tell you pretty closely if your grip pressure is correct. It works on a scale of one to ten. Put your hands on the club in the correct manner and hold the club vertically, pointing straight up in the air. Hold the club as lightly as you can, exerting almost no pressure with your hands. That's a one on our scale. Now hold the club as tightly as you can, exerting as much pressure as you can generate. That's ten. Now go up and down the scale, moving gradually from light to tight and from tight to light. For most shots, your grip pressure should be at five or less. You might want it a little lighter, say a three, for a short putt. You might want it a little lighter if you have to hit a ball over a tree and need to make a longer swing with more wrist cock. You might want it tighter, to six or seven, if you have to dig a shot out of heavy rough. But four or five is about right for most other shots.

Normally you want the grip pressure equal in the two hands, but there are times when that changes. If you need to hit a low slice, you need more pressure in your left hand than your right to hold the clubface and keep it from turning over. If you need to hit a hook, lighten up in the left and grip a little more firmly with the right to make the clubface turn over through impact.

Grip pressure is something you can—and should—practice while you're watching television or reading this book or whatever. Practice it enough so that you'll be able to identify the correct pressure instinctively. In a short time, you will easily be able to identify ten distinct grip pressure feels and it will come in handy.

Finally, try to keep that grip pressure constant throughout the swing. You will tighten it instinctively a little as you swing the club back. Try to avoid this. Don't make any change in grip pressure during the change of direction at the top. That's a common fault, and it can do serious damage to your swing.

There are eight basic steps, checkpoints, or positions that my instructors use to make a quick and accurate diagnosis of swing errors. You won't need to learn or refine them all at once. However, when you do learn any of those eight steps, each corrected position should flow into one smooth swing. At this point I want to tell you what they are, in order to give you a foundation on which you can build that swing. This should also help you to identify your swing errors. Then, by using body drills and other drills, you can make the necessary corrections and go about the business of coordinating the motions so they become an effective swinging action.

STEP ONE:

The First Move in the Backswing

Face-on   Down-line

Moving the club the first three feet away from the ball is a critical move that, if done correctly, lets the remainder of the swing fall into place more easily.

It is the one area of the swing in which there is little room for personal preference. Actually, I'm somewhat fanatical about this. By starting off properly, you put yourself at a huge advantage. You're off to a good start, and it is a move you can repeat.

Starting the club back actually should begin with a slight move forward. I often refer to this as a micromove, because it is so small. You can make this micromove in several ways, although I often recommend lifting the right heel slightly and returning it to the ground to trigger your backswing. I frown on a forward press with the hands, because it gets the hands too active in the takeaway. The ignition move is slightly forward, then you rebound into the backswing. It's very athletic. It reduces tension and promotes flow.

The first move back should be a one-piece action in which everything—shoulders, arms, hands, hips, and club—moves together. With many golfers we recommend just a slight move with the left leg, generally a nudge off the left instep. Most players will feel the upper body controlling the initial move. This is okay if at the same time the weight moves slightly off the left foot and begins to move onto the inside of the right and toward the heel. Many golfers will do well to feel the movement in the feet. The club then moves back almost involuntarily, with no attempt to guide or rotate it, while the shaft stays between the arms. The hands are used only to maintain feel as the club rises naturally along the backward arc. The hands should sense but not dominate. Remember, there should be no manipulation of the club with the hands and no immediate cocking of the wrists.

Your hands and arms should be free of tension, and your body remains level, with no dipping or raising. Creating a true swinging action will set or cock your wrists naturally. You won't have to worry about when or where to set them.

At this early stage the right leg becomes the backswing pivot point, the post you will turn on. Be sure to maintain the flex in your right knee. It is often useful to think of this first move away from the golf ball as a movement to the side rather than a turn, which can create a reverse pivot.

Using the big muscles, especially the arms and shoulders and not the hands and wrists, at this stage of the backswing ensures that there will be no jerky motions but rather a smooth pace that establishes a good tempo for the whole swing. Remember, you have just started the golf club away. It's only moved a few feet.

The Waggle

The old Scottish proverb "As ye waggle, so shall ye swing" is good to remember. The waggle is your preparatory movements of the club, hands, wrists, and arms. I bring it up at this juncture to remind you of its importance. The waggle occurs before the swing and before the micromove ignition. It is another guard against freezing over the ball. Every golfer has his or her own waggle, so there are no absolutes. Remember, however, that your waggle should be a minirehearsal of whatever type of shot you plan to play. The waggle sets the tone for the upcoming shot. It's actually part of the preshot routine, which I cover in detail later in this section.

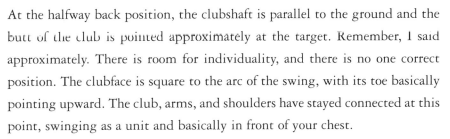

STEP TWO:
Halfway Back

At the halfway back position, the clubshaft is parallel to the ground and the butt of the club is pointed approximately at the target. Remember, I said approximately. There is room for individuality, and there is no one correct position. The clubface is square to the arc of the swing, with its toe basically pointing upward. The club, arms, and shoulders have stayed connected at this point, swinging as a unit and basically in front of your chest.

Most of your weight has now shifted to the right foot, and you should have the same amount of flex in your right knee as when you started, although the knee is not rigid. Your clubhead is now as far away from the tar-

Face-on

Down-line

get as it should ever be. Your left knee should remain flexed and is now flexing inward as the hips have begun to turn. Your right arm remains above your left. That's a rule I've used forever. If it is under your left, you have either rolled your forearms or swung the club too far inside the target line or committed an all-arms takeaway—or all three. In any case, in my book this is a death move. Correct this immediately.

If the clubface at this stage is too shut—pointing too much toward the ground—you have manipulated the club with your hands or made an excessively steep shoulder turn. I'm much more concerned with the rolled-open clubface. Overrotation of the clubface (fanning the club open) is a terrible mistake. Again, avoid this move at all costs.

That said, there can be some deviation in the clubface and/or shaft positions here. Some top players, like Ray Floyd and Bruce Lietzke, take the club inside at this point. Others, like Lee Trevino, Fred Couples, and Curtis Strange, take it outside. But all are able to make the proper corrections during the downswing. If you can do that too, don't tinker with any slight deviations at Step Two.

Face-on   Down-line

When the backswing is three-quarters complete, your left arm should be approximately parallel to the ground and reasonably straight, but not stiff. It also should be close to parallel to the target line. That means not pulled across your chest or lifted away from your body.

At this juncture, your wrist cock should be nearly complete, with the clubshaft at approximately a right angle to your left arm, forming what we call the L position. The club should feel light at this point. Some great players, like Nick Faldo and Seve Ballesteros, cock the club earlier. Some, like Jack Nicklaus, Fred Couples, Tiger Woods, Greg Norman, and Davis Love III, delay finishing the wrist cock until closer to the top of the swing. But at least for iron shots, a right angle at this stage is the norm.

Your left wrist should not have rolled or twisted here, because that takes the club off the correct plane. Believe me, it's easy to make this mistake. In a model swing, the left wrist should be nearly flat, in line with your left forearm, and the clubface should be in line with your wrist. That's because your right wrist has cocked back and put you into a strong hitting position. Remember, don't worry about minor deviations as long as the swing is working. The backswing club action can be far overrated. It's the body coil that is more crucial, because if the body is in position, many swing errors are corrected in the transition from backswing to downswing.

You should feel very much in balance, with your weight slightly on the inside of the right foot and toward the heel (never toward the toes), and your right knee has retained its flex. Your grip pressure should be equal in both hands and at about four or five on our grip scale. Try to maintain the grip pressure you had at address. It will tend to increase slightly as you take the club away. Don't let that happen. Constant grip pressure is critical to a good golf swing. Tightening up will destroy everything.

One last point: your chin will have likely rotated to the right and/or your head has shifted slightly to the right. But the eyes remain focused on the ball, at least in a general way.

STEP FOUR:

The Top of the Backswing

Face-on

Down-line

Swinging from Step Three to the top of the backswing is basically a matter of momentum. At Step Four, the upper body has completed its windup and, ideally, the lower body has already initiated the downswing. As in all athletic throwing or hitting actions, the lower body makes the first shift movement, so there is no specific moment at which the backswing ends and the forward swing begins. The club is actually going back as the lower body goes forward. I point this out simply as a fact, but I recommend that you don't think about it. It's a negative swing thought for many golfers.

The length of your full backswing depends on your physique and flexibility. Thus, your 100 percent shoulder turn probably will be different from others'. Turn your shoulders so you feel that they are fully wound. You should feel a little tension or tightness in your left latissimus dorsi muscles. However, don't overturn, because that can throw you out of balance, create a reverse pivot, and cause other problems. Many amateurs we see do overturn. In fact, my general observation is that amateurs use too much body action in the backswing and not enough on the forward swing. Professionals do just the opposite!

In a full swing, your shoulders should turn between approximately 75 and 100 degrees, maybe a little farther if you're very supple and can do so without overextending. Mentally and ideally, your hips should turn about half that much. At the top, your left shoulder should be behind the ball, approximately in line with the inside of your right leg. Your weight should be toward the heel of the right foot and about on the center of the foot, never to the outside or toward the toes.

Your right knee remains flexed, not rigid, and your left knee should be pointed slightly behind the ball. It's okay for the left heel to come off the ground slightly, as long as your pivot pulls it off. Never consciously lift it. A good thought is to roll the weight to and off the inside of your left foot as you swing back. Good, rhythmic footwork on the backswing is essential. Thinking of the golf swing as a dance step can help a lot. Think of improving your swing as learning a dance step and improve on your footwork. It will automatically help your rhythm and timing sequence.

At the top, your head will have moved to its maximum, and will have rotated probably somewhere between 20 and 45 degrees, and may have also shifted to the right. That's all right; I'll talk more about that later. Your left arm should be firm but not stiff. Slightly bent at the elbow is okay. Trying to keep that left arm rigid adds . . . well, rigidity, runoff, and tension.

Keep the hands quiet. Don't try to pick up extra backswing length and power by extending the arms and hands after your body has quit turning. That disconnects the club from the swing center and usually results in disaster. An idea we use at the schools is that when the shoulders stop winding, the arms stop swinging.

STEP FIVE:
Moving Down to the Ball

Face-on   Down-line

Assuming that you have done things reasonably well on the backswing, here is the make-or-break area of the swing. I said earlier that ideally the lower body initiates the forward swing before the upper body finishes going back, so there is no stopping or starting point as you begin the move down to the ball. The reason I almost never use this as a swing thought for my students is that it conjures up a quick move. Actually the arms and hands are passive, essentially in free fall from the top, responding to the movement of the lower body. The right shoulder and the right elbow drop into their proper slots in response to the hips and legs shifting laterally and the hips also turning in the forward swing. As the club lowers to about waist height, the feeling is that the right elbow is glued to the right side while the left arm is fully extended and pulling. *Pull is a feel, not an intentional swing thought.* That's a response to the action of the body, not a conscious manipulation. Your arms and the club are still connected to the body motion, responding to it, rather than having the hands independently throw the club. At the halfway point down, the shaft is in much the same position as it was in Step Three, except that the arc is narrower and the shaft is closer to the target than when you took the club back. The wrists are still cocked. If the forward swing is initiated by an outward movement of the right shoulder, as is often the case, or by an independent movement of the arms and hands, you will probably be coming down from outside the target line and "casting" the club, which means the hands will release too soon and on the wrong path.

At this point your weight has shifted diagonally left and your hips have shifted laterally toward the target, an automatic response to the fact that the feet and legs have initiated the downswing. When I speak about "lateral," I'm referring here to just a small shift. It's a little move but tremendously important. Your right knee has kicked forward toward the ball or at target line, and there is a small space between your knees looking down the target line. The right knee does not slide down the inside railroad track. Think about that and practice this move. Your head is at or slightly behind the address position. Your right heel is slightly off the ground, and your left knee is forward of your left hip, more or less in a straight line with the middle of your left foot, still flexed but in the process of straightening.

Now the geometry or positioning of the shaft is much more important than it was when you took the club away. The shaft should be on plane, aligned parallel to the target line. The butt of the club should be pointing at your target line. If it falls below this plane, you will push, hook the ball, or hit behind it. If it is above or outside this plane, a toe hit and a weak slice probably will result. With an iron, this is also a good prelude to a shank! As instructors, we can predict very accurately where the ball will go here at Step Five.

As you deliver the club to the ball, your shoulders are unwinding rapidly and are catching up to the turning of the hips. This means the clubhead is behind or trailing your body.

If you are someone who slices the ball, it may help to get into this position by feeling that you are slowing down the turn back to the ball. I tell slicers to slow down the "target turn." This is your turn back to the golf ball. This helps to deliver the golf club from the inside.

Remember, as the lower body starts the downswing, the arms and hands are in free fall from the top. The sequence of movements from the top of the backswing is absolutely critical to consistently solid ball-striking. First shift (or bump the left hip), then rotate and lower the club into the delivery position. Practice this move and I'll guarantee you will improve. Check yourself in front of a mirror.

STEP SIX:
Impact

Many good and great players have swings that look unusual, even weird. Jim Furyk, David Duval, Miller Barber, Gay Brewer, and Nancy Lopez are some prime examples. They all take the club up in a very unusual fashion before self-correcting and swinging it back down on the correct plane. Lee Trevino

Face-on   Down-line

is not exactly what we would call orthodox, and yet he and Ben Hogan are regarded as the top two ball-strikers of the twentieth century. Bruce Lietzke, Lanny Wadkins, Raymond Floyd, and a host of others I could mention all have highly individualistic golf swings. Yet all have one thing in common— when they return to impact, they're perfect for the shot pattern they play. As someone once said, "You don't want to hit the ball with Lee Trevino's back-swing, you want to hit it with his downswing."

At impact, each has the clubface square, the angle of approach on the correct path and the correct plane, the center of the clubface contacting the ball, and the clubhead traveling at high speed. The left and right hands are working together as a unit, not fighting each other, the body has turned and shifted properly, and everything is in wonderful balance.

This is not to say that you should ignore the fundamentals I have outlined in Steps One through Five. Those great players just execute them a little differently, because each of them and all the other good players with swings that don't match the mold have marvelous athletic skills. This is the main reason I came up with the concept of swing corridors—to allow for

57

human differences and natural talent. All of those great players swing within those corridors of success, even though it might not look like it. Well, maybe not Miller Barber, but there are always exceptions, even to the broadest of rules.

You can vary too within those parameters, as long as you have the ability to get back to impact the way they do. But I'd recommend that you heed these guidelines to get back to that proper impact alignment. That's the real moment of truth, which is the culmination of everything that went before in the swing.

At impact, then, you want to look like this:

The left wrist should be slightly arched or bowed, not collapsing and bending inward. That, my friends, is one true golf fundamental. The right wrist should be angled backward to match the flat left wrist instead of hinged forward—this means the two hands are working together. The shaft should be lined up with the left arm, not the right arm. If the hands slow down through impact or if you overaccelerate the club with your right hand, you lose both power and direction.

The weight is mainly on the left leg and foot, more toward the heel. On longer shots, the right heel has come off the ground, and the right knee has fired forward to about the center of your body. A good swing key is to feel that you are bringing your hands and right knee back to the ball together. The left knee is still slightly flexed, and there is a space between the knees.

The right elbow is still very close to the right hip and is still slightly bent. The right arm will straighten out through the impact zone, providing additional thrust through the shot.

The turning of the shoulders still has not caught up with the turning of the hips. After their initial lateral move, the hips have cleared well to the left, about 30 degrees or so. The shoulders also are just slightly left or open, about 10 to 20 degrees, at impact. Be sure not to carry the lateral motion of the hips too far—they will move laterally naturally as the lower body initiates the downswing and then will turn. This rotation or clearing to the left is vital to a good swing.

The body stands up a little through the impact, because we move against the ground to gain leverage and power. A good thought for most of our school attendees is to keep the left shoulder high through impact. This stops the "over the top" comeover tendency. If the student has too much lag or is too much inside out, we go with the opposite feel. Right side high, left shoulder low.

STEP SEVEN:

The Early Follow-Through

Face-on

Down-line

Everything that happens from now on is pretty much a result of what you did in Steps One through Six, but there are some follow-through thoughts that you can use in practice to actually improve the earlier actions.

Step Seven is the portion of the swing between impact and the point at which your right arm is parallel to the ground. The problems I see here commonly involve the left arm overextending to the target, which causes a disconnection with the left side and eventually a breakdown of the left wrist, or the left arm sawing across the body and breaking down.

When the club reaches the halfway-through position parallel to the ground, the elbows and forearms should be almost level with each other. In the last stage of this position, as the clubshaft points skyward, it should almost extend from the line of the right arm with only a slight angle at the wrist. Many golfers are much too wristy or flippy through the shot—that, or the arms collapse into the body.

Don't let your footwork and legwork break down at this point. Your feet and legs should still be active, and your hips should still be turning as your weight moves eventually to the point where it is totally on your left leg. This rotation keeps the club and body center connected.

And don't try to keep your head still and your eyes focused on the impact point. Your head should come up and your eyes should follow the ball once it is away. So don't focus on "head down," as so many high handicappers tend to do. It's bad medicine and will only inhibit your progress.

STEP EIGHT:
Finish and Rebound

Face-on   Down-line

Again, if you have done things right before, the momentum of your swing will carry you to a full, balanced finish position. At the completion of your swing, your hips and shoulders are fully rotated, with your stomach facing to the left of the target and your right shoulder closer to the target than your left, and the club is momentarily behind your head, its plane basically matching the plane of your shoulders. Your weight is completely on the left foot, toward the heel, and your right foot is up on its toe. At this point, you ought to be able to stand on the left foot and tap your right foot on the ground.

From finish you rebound the golf club into a relaxed, balanced position in front of your body, your hands at about chest height, as you watch the flight of the ball. Again, the weight stays on the left foot (tap your right foot just to make sure) as you hold the position and evaluate your shot. This gives you a sense of balance at the finish, feel for where your body should be at the finish, and feedback as you watch the shot that your swing has produced. "Hold and Evaluate" is a term we have coined at our schools.

Putting the Eight Steps to Work

Those are the steps, the eight positions we carefully check as your body, arms, hands, and club move through the swing. You can and should examine and practice individual steps. But eventually you must understand that each of these separate positions is not a stopping point. These are positions you move through. The eight positions become one, blended together in a smooth, rhythmic, effortless swing that produces the long, accurate shots you're after.

Let's look at some ways we can accomplish that.

BODY DRILLS

To get the feeling of the full swing motion, start without a club. First, take your stance and lay a club on the ground perpendicular to your body, so it bisects your stance. Stand over the shaft as it splits your body. One half of

The Eight-Step Swing, Face-On

1. The first move in the backswing

2. Halfway back

3. Three-quarter backswing position

4. Top of the backswing

5. The first move down

6. Impact

7. The early follow-through

8. Finish

(*Tony Roberts*)

1.

2.

5.

6.

3.

4.

7.

8.

The Eight-Step Swing, Down-Line

1. The first move in the backswing

2. Halfway back

3. Three-quarter backswing position

4. Top of the backswing

5. The first move down

6. Impact

7. The early follow-through

8. Finish

(*Tony Roberts*)

1.

2.

5.

6.

3.

4.

7.

8.

your body is on one side of the shaft, the other on the other side. Next, assume your correct posture, bending from the hip and flexing your knees, then cross or fold your arms over your chest. Now simply coil your upper body to the right over a fairly resistant lower body. Visualize yourself in a cylinder or tube that is consistent with your spine angle at address, and coil within that imaginary tube. Turn so the buttons on the front of your shirt are over the inside of your right leg, keeping your weight to the inside of the right leg, with your right knee maintaining the flex it had at address. You should feel some tension in the left latissimus dorsi muscle and on the inside of your right knee. This is a very simple, efficient motion when it is executed properly. However, I know from a ton of experience that it takes practice. So do this move in front of a mirror until you can make a good-looking back coil. You'll know it when you see it.

Your shoulders rotate around the spine at a constant 90-degree angle to the spine. If you were standing straight up, your shoulder turn would be perfectly level. But since your spine is tilted forward, the shoulders will turn at a slight tilt. Your right shoulder feels like it goes up and behind you. This is an important visual that can really help you. You should feel that the left shoulder is getting behind the golf ball. I prefer to have students feel that the left shoulder stays level as opposed to going down. On the forward swing, your shoulders essentially rotate in the other direction around the spine, which is on a tilt. In truth, the right shoulder is lower and the left shoulder is higher at impact than they were at address. It's important for golfers to understand what they should be trying to accomplish. This simple realization can do wonders for many people.

 ## HEAD MOVEMENT

Should your head move to the right on the backswing? It's a fact that most top players' heads do. "Keep your head still" is another of those golf adages that really don't happen. If you keep your head totally still and try to rotate your body around your spine with this fixed pivot point (which some instructors still teach), you'll probably end up making a reverse pivot, with your weight sinking into your left foot. That's definitely not where you want to be on the backswing. It's a true death position in my book. There are just a couple of things you can do from there. One is to keep going forward on the downswing, which means you will probably find the ball with the hosel of the club. That's called a shank. The best you can do with that motion is reverse back in the forward swing producing very little power and very little accuracy. Remember since you're forward on the backswing, you go backward on the forward swing. As you can imagine, that doesn't produce much in the way of an acceptable shot. To sum it up, if you succeed in not moving your head at all, you'll have a tension-dominated backswing, and it will be unlike the backswing of any player on any tour anywhere.

As you coil your upper body, be careful to maintain your spine angle. That means keeping your spine tilted the same amount at the finish of your backward coil as it was at address. Losing the spine angle is a common problem. Sometimes players dip going back, which means their spine drops. Usually they will then raise up and lose the angle in the other direction. Some players will raise up in the backswing, making a very flat shoulder turn. It's very important to keep that spine angle constant, because that maintains the club's reference to the ground and the ball.

Another common fault, which I touched on earlier, is trying to make too big a turn, which usually results in overturning the hips and knees (and the knees getting too close together). A number of years ago I wrote a book called *The X-Factor Swing.* I also did a videotape and ran a ten-part series on the Golf Channel in which I examined how the difference between your shoulder turn and your hip turn affects your power and the distance you can hit the ball. Working with a company called SportSense, we found that the greater the difference between those two turns, the farther you can hit the ball. If you let your hips and knees turn along with the shoulders, you're cre-

Body Drill

The body drill is
essentially the same as
one of your warm-up
drills, only this time
your arms are folded
across your chest.
Assume your setup
position (1), coil fully
into your backswing
position (2), return
through impact (3), and
go into the finish
position (4). Be sure to
keep your spine angle
intact in positions 1
through 3.
(*Tony Roberts*)

1.

2.

3.

4.

ating no resistance to the winding of the upper body. That means you get less torque at the top, which translates into less speed going forward and less distance. As I said earlier, in a power backswing the shoulders generally turn about twice as much as the hips, the hips twice as much as the knees. You should try to come as close as you can to this rule of thumb if you want to increase your X and gain more power.

Practice the simple, efficient coiling of the upper body over a resistant lower body, all the while maintaining your spine angle. Turn back until you can't turn your upper body any more.

Having wound up efficiently, now you want to go forward, and this is where I see most players having trouble. The correct sequence of motion is the same as in any other stick-and-ball sport or throwing motion—to throw something fast or hit something hard, you need to shift weight to the front leg. That means something from your lower center (stomach area) down has to move first. The upper body stays coiled, at least momentarily. You can feel that you are shifting your weight with your left foot or knee or hip, or that you are pushing off the inside of your right foot and leg—whatever works best for you. This concept works for at least 90 percent of the people attending our schools.

Try it. Make a small weight shift to the left. You can see that as your hips move laterally, your right shoulder naturally rocks down. You can also try the reverse. That is, start the right shoulder down and the left hip will automatically bump forward. Now try unwinding your upper body first. The right shoulder goes out and around, which means the club is going to do the same. This produces an outside-to-inside swing path, which means the clubhead will be coming into the ball from outside the target line. The result will usually be a pull or even a shank, certainly at the very least a weak, glancing blow. Yet this is how, in our schools and everywhere else, we see a great majority of the people playing golf.

Let's take a closer look at the lower-body action. We hear a lot of talk about rotation, rotation, rotation. This implies that there is no lateral motion

Keep your spine angle intact
throughout the backswing
(1) and through impact.
Don't drop down (2) or raise
up (3) as you swing back.
(*Tony Roberts*)

1.

Yes

2.

No

3.

No

in the swing. That's simply not the case. Yes, it's important to rotate the lower body, but that rotation has to be preceded by a lateral movement. Anybody who tells you that there is no lateral motion has simply not studied videotape or watched what good players do. I suspect the myth was born and continues to live because a lot of very good players tend to have too much lateral motion. Tom Kite was one in his earlier years. He is one player I'm very familiar with who has battled this problem. Very good players tend to produce swing paths that are too much inside to out because they have too much leg action. We used to be told that the more we hit it left, the more we should drive our legs so we wouldn't hit it left. Actually, just the opposite is usually the case. The old-time teaching was "drive your legs, keep your head back, and square the club with your hands." So a lot of the players of today grew up like that, and we see a lot of excessive motion—or players trying to get rid of that excessive motion. I've often talked to Nick Price on the range at Doral, and he feels that in his mind his left hip goes straight back on his forward swing. Yet we know from video that he has one of the biggest lateral motions on Tour. So what you feel and what you really do can be quite different. I hate to say it, but it's a good idea never to listen to what any Tour player tells you about his swing. Almost always it will not relate to your game, and the swing that person is using may be countering an excessive temporary problem. Next month he or she will be working on something entirely different.

So your lower-body action has to become a matter of feel, to coordinate that lateral movement with the rotation that follows. As the noted teacher Bob Toski has said, the swing is simply "turn, shift, and turn." So coil your upper body onto your right post, shift your weight to your left post, and then unwind your body all the way to an upright finish. At the finish, your trunk is pretty much straight up and down. The old "reverse C" often promotes hanging back through impact and is hard on the back. That said, a slight reverse C is still okay with me—just nothing that damages your back or encourages a hangback. Your knees at the finish are fairly close together. Your weight is on your left leg, and your right foot is on its toe. At this point, notice how much of your body is behind the shaft on the ground. I hope it will be almost none. If you have finished correctly, the only part of your body not in front of the shaft is your right foot. Everything else is in front. And you should be in balance, able to hold that finish. The good players check their balance by holding their finishes. I call it a "resistance point." You don't necessarily have to hold your full follow-through long, because there can be a rebound effect at the end of the swing. You can bring your arms and hands back down in front of you. But you should be able to hold your body position indefinitely.

Actually, it's a very simple motion, and all of our students get it with just a little practice. We repeat it every day of each school for at least ten-minute segments. Players come to our schools all the time thinking that we are going to add a lot of things to their swings. On the contrary, what we usually try to do is take things out, especially when it comes to body movement. Remember, the simpler and more efficient your body motion is, the better you will play!

A similar drill is to go through the same exercise, but this time, instead of crossing your arms over your chest, hold a club across the back of your neck. This is similar to one of the warm-up drills you learned earlier. Now go through the same routine—get into a good setup position, coil your upper body behind the imaginary ball, then shift to the left and unwind, smoothly and efficiently. Do it again, only this time stop at the impact position and check the alignment of your shoulders and hips. Your shoulders should be pretty square to the target line, maybe slightly open, and your hips should be open even more. Most amateurs do it exactly the opposite—their hips are pretty square and their shoulders are open when they strike the ball. That creates an out-to-in swing path, an off-center hit, and a slice.

Next we want to add the arms to the motion. Assume your good posture and let your arms hang. Imagine you are holding a grapefruit in your

1.

3.

2.

Body Drill with Shaft

Assume your setup position without a club, with your arms
hanging freely and a shaft bisecting your feet (1). Swing back (2)
and through (3), making sure that only your right foot is behind
the shaft at the finish. (*Tony Roberts*)

73

The Grapefruit Drill

Set up to the ball and imagine you are holding a grapefruit in your hands (1), or touch your thumbs together to ensure that your hands don't fly apart during the swing. Now swing back (2) and through (3), coordinating the swinging of your arms with the movements of your body. Do it again and stop at impact (4) to check your position.

(*Tony Roberts*)

1.

2.

3.

4.

hands (or you can touch your thumbs together). We do this so your arms don't fly apart at the top of the backswing. Allow your elbows to bend a little as you do this drill. I like the forearms hanging at a 45-degree angle. Now make the same body motion, only this time your arms will travel along with the body coil. Keep your arms in front of your body center. The arms swing in concert with the movement of the body. They don't run off on their own. As you coil back, the arms swing with you. Shift and unwind and allow the arms to sail through to the finish. Do it again, but this time stop at impact to check your shoulder and hip positions. Are you achieving the impact alignments you are striving for? Then swing on through to the finish. Now swing back, stop at the top, swing down to impact and stop, then swing through to the finish. You can do variations of this to check your positions throughout the swing.

THE RIGHT ARM: A JIM McLEAN GOLF SCHOOL FUNDAMENTAL

Let me explain how the right arm works in the swing, and in doing so clear up another myth. At one time, we were taught to tuck the right arm in and keep the right elbow close to the body on the backswing. Teachers used to tell their students to tuck a handkerchief or a headcover under their right arm and not to let it fall out during the swing. That's not happening anymore. The right elbow starts off of your body at setup and stays off of your body in the backswing. Many golfers do well to feel that the right arm goes away from the body on the backswing and comes back in to the body on the downswing, just as it does when you throw a rock into a lake or do any other throwing or hitting activity. To me, the action of the right arm is the most important ally any right-handed golfer can have, if it is used correctly. Why not use your most coordinated and powerful hand and arm? Most people can do things much better with their dominant side. So can you. We just have to

Right Arm
Only Drill

Set up with your left hand on your chest (1) and swing with your right arm without a club. Let the right arm swing wide going back, the elbow coming away from the shoulder (2). On the downswing, the right arm returns close to the body through impact (3) and away from the body again on the follow-through and finish (4).

(*Tony Roberts*)

1.

2.

3.

4.

train your right arm to do the proper motion. Ken Venturi once likened it to the brushstroke you use when painting a wall. Picture that in your mind and you'll have a pretty good image of the right-arm action. Brush up in the backstroke and brush down in the forward stroke. Visualize a paintbrush in your right hand and you will catch on to this concept very quickly.

If you keep your right arm tucked in, what's going to happen to the left arm? It will have to bend, or it will have to swing across your chest in a very flat plane. You'll be unable to get full extension and a wide arc on the backswing. When Jack Nicklaus first caught the public's eye in the late '50s and early '60s, he was criticized for his "flying right elbow." All Jack was doing was letting the right elbow stay in position. Rather than tuck it in, he used a wide extension and a more upright swing plane. This wide arc helped Jack become arguably the greatest driver of the golf ball in the twentieth century, and certainly the greatest player in history.

We want our school attendees to feel wide on the backswing and then narrow on the downswing—that is a fundamental with every swing on the PGA Tour, the Senior PGA Tour, and the LPGA Tour, and with every good player. Nobody is taking it back narrow and bringing it down wide—which is, by the way, what many higher handicappers and short hitters do on every swing.

I encourage you to do any or all of these three body drills for several minutes a day, three or four days a week, in front of a mirror if possible. If you're outside, do these and any practice swings with the sun directly at your back, so you can see your shadow on the ground and immediately detect any incorrect movements. If you do them correctly for just that little amount of time, you will get better at golf.

PATH AND PLANE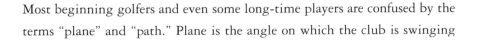

Most beginning golfers and even some long-time players are confused by the terms "plane" and "path." Plane is the angle on which the club is swinging

Right Arm with Club Drill

Swinging a club with the right arm only trains you to use that arm well. The procedure is the same as the Right Arm Only drill, only this time you have a club in your hand. Swing wide going back (1), narrow coming down (2) and through impact (3), and wide again through (4) to the finish (5). (*Tony Roberts*)

1.

2.

3.

4.

5.

in relation to the ground and the target line. Path is the direction the club-head travels, back and through, in relation to the target.

Let's go back to that big clock on the ground, with the target line running from six to twelve. Your clubhead will sit on that line and the shaft will angle to the inside, or toward nine o'clock (just the opposite if you're a left-hander). The angle of the shaft when the clubhead is properly soled is essentially the angle or plane on which the club should swing, at least from waist height to waist height. When we do our video analyses in our schools, we draw a line along the shaft and extend it upward, bisecting the body somewhere just below the belt line. It's as if that line were the roof of a house and you are standing in the attic, with your head outside the roof. In his book *Five Lessons: The Modern Fundamentals of Golf,* Ben Hogan used a pane of glass with his head sticking through it to illustrate the correct plane. However, this plane is very different from the shaft plane. It corresponds to your left arm and not the shaft. Yet it is a great visual, and I use this wonderful visual concept with many golfers. I refer to this as "the Hogan plane," while our instructors usually look more closely at the shaft plane. The shaft plane tells us much more about the clubhead and clubshaft arc.

There are no straight lines in a good golf swing. We're not trying to take the club straight back over six o'clock or straight ahead to twelve. In a golf swing, the club whirls and orbits around the body in a circle that is laid on an angle. That angle is called the swing arc. Remember, there are no straight lines in a circle. (Note: With lateral motion, you widen the arc at the bottom of the swing. I term this "the flat spot" in the swing. Lateral shift allows the club to travel near the target line longer.)

Now, you have fourteen clubs in your bag. Each has a different angle and weight, and each is a different length, so you can see that things might get a little complicated. The good news is that each club, leaning at its pre-determined angle, will seek the proper arc if we create a true swinging action. If we don't lift it or pull it or otherwise leverage it, the club will swing on its own correct plane. In other words, the pitching wedge has an upright lie, which is the angle of the shaft in relation to the bottom of the club and the ground, so the shaft will be standing more vertically. This will dictate a more vertical or upright swing plane. It's also a short club and you are in close to the wedge, again encouraging an upright swing arc. The driver has the flattest lie of any club, and you're standing farther away from it. This dictates a flatter plane and a more rounded swing, which is what you want with that club. So if you truly create a swinging action, the club will seek the proper plane and you really won't have to worry much about plane. Think of it this way: Studying the swing plane is good for teachers. It's probably good for students to grasp the concept. But for playing the game, "plane details" can ruin the swing. Nothing is more important than learning to swing.

And again there is room for individuality. Since 1991 at the Doral-Ryder Open, we have taped the swings of every player in the tournament. As we have studied players taking the club back, we see that about one third are under the so-called ideal plane, about one third are on it, and about one third are over it. That's why I've stated that the backswing is often overrated and

The Plane Truth

The club does not swing straight back and through from six o'clock to twelve o'clock. The plane on which each club swings is basically determined by its lie, or the angle of the shaft with the ground.

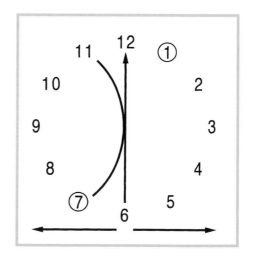

exact positioning is not critical. But coming down, at about waist height, every Tour player who is playing well has the club on that ideal plane. That's simply the geometry of good shot-making. You are either on plane, under the plane, or over the plane, and the plane determines direction, contact, and power. So as long as you stay within the parameters I've outlined, the correct plane is only a benchmark, not an absolute, on the backswing. Then, by using the proper sequence of motion going forward—shift, rotate, hit—combined with a true swing action, you will cause your golf club to begin to fall on plane. You will never break the pane of glass Hogan visualized.

Path, as I said, is the direction the clubhead travels back and through. I've talked about not wanting to take the club too far inside or too far outside going back. A little of either is all right as long as you can correct it coming down. Using our clock model, on the downswing, the clubhead ideally approaches the ball from seven and swings out toward one. That's what I call an inside attack track. The clubhead really doesn't go across the target line and out to one, but your feeling is that from your vantage point, the clubhead should be traveling from seven toward one. As you come through the impact zone, the clubface will be closing and your forearms rotating. We call that covering the ball. It's an idea I got from Jimmy Ballard more than twenty years ago, and now many top players use that term to describe the correct striking action. Your whole right side plus the clubface covers.

Why not approach the ball from six o'clock, swinging the club toward twelve, to hit it dead straight? That's a Ferris wheel swing, and many golfers incorrectly carry this image to the golf course. That would be logical if you had a putter in your hands and your eyes were over the target line. But with all other clubs, you are standing to the side of the target line, so the club must come off that line, swinging back and swinging through. For most of our students, I really don't want them to hit the ball straight. Straight is actually very confining. It's a double don't—don't curve it to the right and don't curve it to the left. I'd rather have a single do. For all juniors and most

The five-iron will swing
on a plane different
from the driver or the
nine-iron. The critical
factor is to be on that
plane about halfway into
the downswing.
(*Tony Roberts*)

1.

2.

5.

6.

3.

4.

7.

8.

amateurs, I'd prefer them to learn to hit a draw, a shot that starts a little right of the target and curves back left toward the target.

Let's take driving as an example. If you try to hit a straight shot, you'll aim it down the middle of a 30-yard fairway, which means you have only a 15-yard margin of error in either direction. But if you know you can consistently curve the ball from right to left, you can aim down the right side of the fairway, and now you have 30 yards to work with before you run out of short grass. A straight drive keeps you in the right corner of the fairway. Your planned draw center-cuts the fairway, while overdrawing (hooking) the ball still gives you a chance to stay on the left side of the fairway. The same thing applies if you consistently fade or curve the ball from left to right. Many great players, such as Nicklaus, Trevino, and Fred Couples, have done this by setting up well left at address. This helps them hit a power fade and not a weak slice when the clubhead approaches the ball from five o'clock and swings to eleven. You can work on that shot too, because you never know when you'll have to slice a ball around a tree. As I pointed out earlier, a lot of great players have faded and do fade the ball. But a fade tends to go higher and doesn't run as far (which is why many top players love it). And that's fine if you can hit it far enough to afford to lose some distance. I suspect that you can't. For most golfers, the longest fade is usually well short of the draw, so that right-to-left action is what I recommend you develop and work on until it becomes second nature.

Fundamentals of Flight

 **WHAT YOUR DIVOTS TELL YOU**

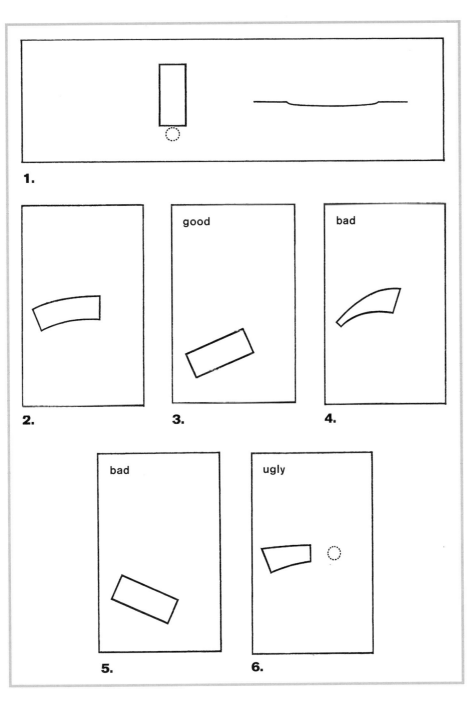

You can tell a lot about your swing by examining your divot after making a shot. The perfect divot (1) is shallow and square, which means the entire bottom of the club has contacted the ground while the club is traveling straight down the target line. A great divot (2) is one that starts straight and turns slightly left, which means the club has started to swing back to the inside after impact. A good divot (3) is one that goes left all the way. This flat divot pattern usually produces a slight fade. Bad divots include one that is toe-deep (4), which indicates an exaggerated inside-out swing path with too much hand action, and one that travels out to the right (5). I hate to see that one, since it spells hook with a capital H. An ugly divot is one that starts well in front of the ball's original position, evidence of a thin, low shot (6).

WHY THE BALL TRAVELS THE WAY IT DOES

To learn more about your swing and how to correct faulty tendencies, it's important to know why the ball flies the way it does.

There are only four flight characteristics to a golf shot: (1) distance; (2) trajectory, the up-and-down path a ball travels; (3) initial direction; and (4) curve. And I believe there are six factors that influence that flight: (1) clubhead path at impact; (2) clubface position at impact; (3) squareness of contact; (4) angle of approach, the angle at which your clubhead comes into the ball; (5) clubhead speed; and (6) alignment at address. These are called the ball-flight laws.

If we forget distance and trajectory for a moment, there are only nine ways a ball can travel. It can start straight and go straight, start straight and curve left, or start straight and curve right. It can start to the left, continue straight on that path to the left, curve more to the left, or curve back to the right. It can start to the right and do the same thing—continue straight

Flight Patterns

The starting direction and curvature of a shot depends primarily on the position of the clubface at impact and the path on which the club is traveling. The speed at which the club is traveling also has an influence on these two factors. A ball can start left, continue straight left, hook farther left, or slice back to the right (1). It can start straight, continue straight, or hook or slice (2). It can start right, continue straight right, slice farther right, or hook back to the left (3).

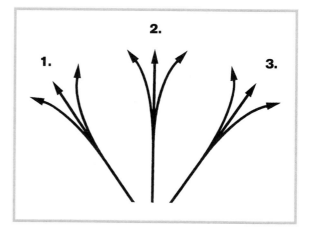

right, curve more right, or curve back to the left. Those facts are immutable. However, it's easy to see that these nine ball-flight paths can have any number of variations, from slight to severe.

The starting direction and curvature of a ball depend primarily on two things—the path on which the clubhead is traveling and the position of the clubface at impact. However, the angle of the clubface is by far the most important. It is also the hardest to control. Research tells us that on a full swing, with the clubhead traveling at a reasonable speed, the ball will start off more in the direction the clubface is pointing. In other words, if your clubhead is traveling straight toward the target at impact and your clubface is 10 degrees open or facing to the right, the ball will start off to the right of the target, and depending upon the angle of attack, center contact, and speed of your swing, it will go more or less right. However, on a short putt, with the putterhead traveling slowly straight to the target but the face closed or pointing left 10 degrees, the ball might start off close to a full 10 degrees left. So clubhead speed absolutely has an influence on starting direction. But the basic premise still applies.

If you swing from outside to inside the target line, the ball may or may not start to the left. If your clubface is square to that outside-in path, the ball will continue straight to the left. To me, clubface is by far the most critical thing to look at. If the clubface is open, your ball is going right. If you're slicing, the clubface is open. Our teachers fix clubface first and then worry about path.

HOW THE LIE OF THE CLUB AFFECTS YOUR SHOT

Essentially, your upper body and arms control the path of the clubhead. The rotation of your hands and forearms, not just your hands, and the turn of your body, control the position of the clubface. Also, your hands hinge going back,

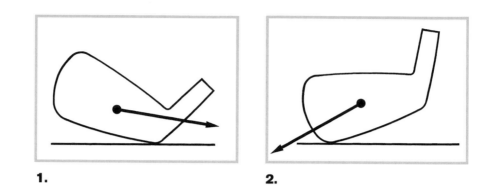

1.   **2.**

**If the lie of a club is incorrect—if it doesn't sit properly on the ground—
deviations in the starting direction of the ball can result. If the club is too
upright, with the toe sticking up too far off the ground (1), the ball will tend to
start to the left. If the club is too flat, with the heel off the ground (2), the ball
will tend to start to the right.**

unhinge through impact, and rehinge on the follow-through. At the same
time, they are rotating with your forearms. The right hand brushes over the
left through impact. That's an image I use over and over. This squares the
clubface at the point of impact, but the rotation continues. It's as if you were
hitting a tennis shot with topspin. Tennis professionals tell you to cover the
ball with the strings of the racket to get topspin. We as golfers are doing the
same thing. The feeling should be that your hands and forearms are covering
the ball as they rotate through impact and into the follow-through. An overrotation before and through the impact area will close the face. An underro-
tation will leave it open.

Knowing that, you can analyze the flight of your shots and pinpoint
whether you have a path problem, a face problem, or both. Having determined why something is happening, you can work on the particular fault or
faults to correct the flight. For example, one of the swing faults we see quite

1.

The right forearm rotates over the left on the downswing, squaring the club at impact and continuing into the follow-through.
(*Tony Roberts*)

2.

3.

The "chicken wing" is when the left elbow flies up and out after impact in a reaction to a path that is too out-to-in or a clubface that is too closed.
(*Tony Roberts*)

No

often is the "chicken wing," which is the left arm and the left elbow sawing across the body up and out after impact instead of swinging out past the ball. The chicken wing is almost always the result of a swing path that is too out-to-in or a clubface that gets too open at impact. Now the player, who has seen the ball go right way too often, is trying desperately to keep the clubface square through impact to make the ball go straight. The problem is, he or she is going at it the wrong way. Almost all the swing faults we see at our schools are the result of players' trying to correct a swing result. They are not curing the true fault.

HOW TO CURVE THE BALL

This knowledge of clubface alignment and path control also helps you curve the ball intentionally, whether by developing that nice little draw that you want or a bigger hook or slice to get around a tree or to come into a tucked flag from the correct direction. If you want a slice around that tree, simply align your feet and body to the left, set your clubface open before you take your grip, and swing normally along your stance line. For a hook, do just the opposite—stand more to the right, close the clubface, and swing along your feet. We preset our desired shot with modified alignments. You can do the same thing with a clubface that is square at address to your starting path, then underrotate or overrotate through impact, but I think presetting the face is more reliable. And always remember the 70 percent rule that influences the direction in which the ball will start. You want to allow enough room to get the ball started around the tree instead of into it. Always remember that the clubface influences both the initial launch direction plus the curve! That's a McLean rule.

Closed (*Tony Roberts*)

Open (*Tony Roberts*)

Square (*Tony Roberts*)

HOW TO CONTROL TRAJECTORY

Your angle of approach, or angle of attack as it is sometimes called, determines to a great extent the height and trajectory of a shot. Golf is sometimes a game of opposites. If you swing down on a ball, you must trust that it will go up. If you swing up on it, you can top it, in which case it will go down right into the ground.

So with the ball on the ground and an iron in your hand, your angle of approach should be slightly downward, striking the ball first and then the turf. This again is a basic fundamental. With the ball on the ground and a fairway wood in your hand, your angle of approach should be basically level, striking the ball first as the wider sole on the wood skids across the grass. With a driver and the ball teed in the air, the ideal approach is level or even slightly upward. The upward approach might launch the ball slightly higher than normal, but because you are applying less spin, the ball will travel on the flatter trajectory you want with a driver. If you swing too steeply down with a driver, however, you will apply much more spin, and the ball will tend to "balloon" on you and fly higher and not as far. We call this an "upshoot" and it is definitely something to avoid.

POSITION THE BALL CORRECTLY

This is where ball position also becomes a factor. With a driver, you want the ball teed opposite your left heel or left instep so you will catch it at or just after the bottom of your swing arc. With a fairway wood, the ball should be played just slightly farther back in your stance. With the longer and middle irons, position it another inch or so back, and play it even farther back with the short irons. We recommend playing it back into the middle of your stance, though. Most weekend amateurs do much better with the ball more centered. It's easier to hit down on all iron shots and also easier to hit from the inside producing the slight draw.

With the driver, the ball should be positioned off the inside of the left heel. (*Tony Roberts*)

With the five-iron, the ball should be positioned a couple of inches back from the left heel.

(*Tony Roberts*)

Ball position must change for different types of shots and hitting off slopes. To hit down on the ball, most people do much better with the ball centered in the stance. By moving the ball forward of center, the bottom of the arc moves closer and closer to the ball until with the driver the swing will be slightly ascending. By changing ball position, you don't have to make any adjustments in your swing other than those that the lie and the length of each club dictate, which you make almost automatically. Don't listen to the books or videos that recommend one ball position for all clubs. Although that may sound logical and simple, it doesn't work for golf. All top players vary ball position. That's a fact.

CATCHING IT ON THE SWEET SPOT

Squareness of contact obviously affects the distance you hit the ball. A ball struck with the club's so-called sweet spot or effective hitting area will go farther than a ball struck off-center, so you'll get your true distance with every club. Striking a ball with the toe or heel also will cause some curvature, even if the clubface is square, because an off-center hit produces a rebound effect on the club at impact, called the "gear effect." This is less true with today's more forgiving clubs, which are bigger and weighted on the perimeter, than it was with the old wooden woods and classic forged iron blades. But it still is a factor. Hitting the ball squarely is certainly a common denominator of all top ball strikers.

SPEED IS THE THING, WITHIN LIMITS

The value of clubhead speed is obvious. The faster your clubhead is traveling at impact, assuming all the other ball-flight factors are in order, the farther you will hit the ball. But don't violate any of the four previous laws in an effort to produce extra speed. Your sentence will be shorter, off-target shots. I'll discuss much more about the subject of speed in "The Power School" chapter.

ALIGNMENTS

One law that is never mentioned in other books definitely affects ball trajectory launch angle and direction. That would be your aim. If you don't aim properly, you can have great path, perfect clubface angle (dead square), the perfect angle of attack, great speed, and center contact. But the ball won't go to your intended target.

THOUGHTS FOR SWINGING

"Drive the ball in the Atlantic Ocean. Try to hit your iron shots on the earth. This as opposed to steering the ball to a target. Don't steer, let go. You have to let go. Playing good golf is like a fine musician playing the piano. He does not try to hit each key. He hears the song in his mind and then he plays the song. There is no conscious thought of what the fingers do."—Jackie Burke

"See the target when you are swinging. Keep an image in your mind consistently. Then don't care where the ball goes."—Manuel de la Torre

These quotes from two great players and teachers I have worked with stay with me at all times as I give lessons and teach golf schools. I hope you will read them again as they have great value, much more than most golfers will ever believe.

THOUGHTS FOR PLAYING

I learned something else from Jackie Burke a long time ago that I've never forgotten. He said golf is basically a game of hitting circles. The first circle is the area in which you're trying to drive the ball. That's a big circle, so you don't have to be that precise and can make a free swing at it. The next circle you're trying to hit is the green, which is also a pretty big target, and you should make a free swing at that too. When you're on the green, you're trying to hit the ball into roughly a 3-foot circle around the cup. Once you get into that 3-foot circle, you putt to the ultimate and smallest circle, the cup. To me, that is great golf thinking. Sometimes when you putt to the 3-foot circle you make it. On the other hand, I think that the notion of trying aggressively to make a putt from 30, 40, 50, or 60 feet is unwise. I like to feel that you're trying to get the ball within that 3-foot circle. That takes a lot of pressure off you, simply because it gives you a bigger area to hit into. And if you get into that area, the smallest circle is a pretty easy target.

Taking pressure off yourself—or not putting pressure on yourself in the first place—is a key to good scoring. Testing has been done to see how close a machine hits a ball at 150 yards, 175, 200, and 225 yards. Even a machine doesn't drop the balls into a neat little pile the size of a towel. It has to contend with the same things a human does—the balls aren't perfect, the shaft isn't perfect, there are wind and other atmospheric factors. The balls end up in a circular pattern, and the size of the circle is about 8 percent of the distance they're being hit—in other words, from 100 yards, you have about an 8-yard circle of balls.

We try to get our students to think in terms of hitting the ball into a circle and not always aiming at the flag. With the hole cut at the edge of a green, even the Iron Byron hitting machine sometimes misses that area. At a particular distance, even the machine is going to miss to the short side occasionally, with the ball kicking down into a water hazard or bunker. And that's off a tee. So depending on the skill level, we'll have students start hitting for the center of the green from every shot outside of, say, 100 yards, 125 yards, or maybe 150 yards. That's something I even use with the Tour players I work with. And of course Jack Nicklaus played his entire career by hitting mostly to the center of the greens in major championships. We go flag-hunting a lot too often, and it severely hurts your scoring ability and your enjoyment of the game.

Dave Collins, my assistant at Sleepy Hollow, had a standing bet with our members that he could take five strokes off a person's score without saying a word on the golf course. He would go out in a cart in front of the group and just take all the flags out. The players wouldn't know where the hole was, so they would just try to hit the ball on the green. Most of the time that's a great way to play. By the way, Dave won his bet every time.

FULL-SWING ERRORS TO AVOID
—the Death Moves

Incorrect Shift

Hanging back or failure to get to your left side

(*Tony Roberts*)

97

MORE FULL-SWING ERRORS TO AVOID
—the Death Moves

Reverse Pivot

Keeping your weight on
your left side and tilting
to the left on your
backswing

(*Tony Roberts*)

Hip Slide

Sliding your hips
laterally on your
backswing instead of
turning (*Tony Roberts*)

Right Leg Bows

Letting your right leg bow outward and destroying your backswing post (*Tony Roberts*)

Right Leg Straightens

Letting your right leg straighten and losing your knee flex on the backswing (*Tony Roberts*)

Head Down at Address

Keeping your head too far down at address, which hinders your ability to swing freely back and through (*Tony Roberts*)

DRILLS TO HELP GROOVE YOUR FULL SWING

Board Under Left Heel

Hit balls with a board under your left heel to quiet an overactive lower body. This freezes the left side, keeps you from spinning out too soon, and helps produce a left-to-right draw. (*Tony Roberts*)

Chair Drill

Sit in a chair or on a stool and hit shots off a tee. This quiets the lower body and encourages a good release through impact. (*Tony Roberts*)

1.

2.

Fan Drill

There are several varieties of fanlike devices that you can swing several times a day to create lag or delay and develop strength. Tom Kite, for one, swings a fan for ten minutes every night.

(*Tony Roberts*)

Yes

Impact Bag

This teaches you the correct impact position. Use a heavy beanbag or similar object and swing into it. Make sure your head is behind the bag, your left arm and shaft are straight, and your left wrist is flat at impact. If you let your upper body slide forward or if the clubhead strikes the bag ahead of the shaft, you have problems. (*Tony Roberts*)

No

Mini-Swing

This was taught to me by Al Mengert. You can also call it the toe-up to toe-up drill. It is one of my staple drills, a real swing builder. Simply swing halfway back (1) and then halfway through (2). This helps you synchronize the movement of the body with the swinging of the arms. The arms do the work, not the hands and wrists. You don't need a lot of flippy hand-and-wrist action to hit the ball a long way.

(*Tony Roberts*)

1.

2.

1. **2.** **3.**

Glove Under Left Arm • This teaches you to keep the upper left arm connected to your chest through impact. Tuck a golf glove under your left arm (1). With a seven-iron, make small swings (2 and 3). The glove should not fall out, at least until you are well into your follow-through. (*Tony Roberts*)

Headcover Under Right Arm

This drill works just the opposite way from the Glove Under Left Arm drill and teaches you to let the right arm swing freely away from the body on the backswing, to gain extension. Put a headcover under your right arm (1). When you swing back to the top, the cover should fall to the ground (2).

(*Tony Roberts*)

1. **2.**

Back to Target

This helps cure a slice and teaches you how to hook the ball, ingraining an inside–down-the-line–inside swing path. Set up with your feet and body aligned about 45 degrees to the right of your target (1). Keep your clubface square to the target. Now hit balls from this setup position, swinging along your body line and rotating the clubface square through impact (2) and into the finish (3).

(*Tony Roberts*)

1.

2.

3.

Left Foot, Right Toe

Set up as shown, the right foot pulled back and on its toe, and swing. This is another excellent antislicing drill. It stabilizes the lower body to prevent spinning out or swinging from outside to in.

(*Tony Roberts*)

1.

2.

Left Foot Back

This is a drill for players who have trouble turning and clearing their left sides on the forward swing. Set up with the left foot pulled back (1), then swing (2), learning the sensation of the left side turning out of the way.

(*Tony Roberts*)

1.

2.

Baseball Swing

Swinging a club like a baseball bat is especially good preshot practice on the course. It gives you the feeling of swinging around your body instead of straight up and down. The feeling of releasing the club through impact becomes ingrained.

(*Tony Roberts*)

105

1.

2.

Pre-Set Drill

If you are having trouble with your
takeaway, assume your address
position and simply hinge your
hands and set the club (1). Then
swing to the top (2) and through to
the finish (3). This presetting gives
you the feeling of having the club
on the correct plane going back.

(*Tony Roberts*)

3.

Feet-Together Drill

Swinging with your feet together is great for promoting balance, rhythm, timing, and good footwork. If you swing too hard or out of rhythm, you'll fall off-balance. (*Tony Roberts*)

Hitchhiking Drill

Make a hitchhiking motion with your left hand and arm. This gives you the feeling of how your left hand and arm should rotate on the forward swing. (*Tony Roberts*)

Throw the Club

This teaches the correct sequence of body movement and arm swing along with the feeling of a correct release. With the club in your right hand, take a couple of steps and simply throw it underhand down the range. Just make sure nobody is nearby when you do it. (*Tony Roberts*)

1.　　　　　**2.**

107

Step-Over Drill

Make your normal swing
(1), and after impact step
with your right foot over
your left (2). This teaches
you to take your right side
out of action and ensures
that you get all your weight
on your left. (*Tony Roberts*)

1.

1.

2.

1.

2.

3.

Return to Impact

This teaches the feeling of correct positions. From address (1), swing back to the top (2). Check to see that your position is correct and you are in balance. Then swing down and stop at impact (3). Check your position to see that your hips are clearing and your weight has gone to the left side and that you are still in balance. You also can stop at other points in the swing to check your position. (*Tony Roberts*)

2.

3.

Impact to Finish

Start at your impact position (1), then swing into the follow-through (2) and on to a balanced finish (3). Check your position at each point. As with the Return to Impact drill, this gives you a feeling for where you should be in the various stages of follow-through and how good your balance is. (*Tony Roberts*)

Slap Drill (*above*)
From your address
position, swing your right
arm back (1), swing down
(2), and slap your left
hand (3). This gives you
the feeling of rotation
through impact with both
your right and left hands
and arms. (*Tony Roberts*)

1.

2.

1.

2.

3.

Five Balls in a Row

This drill encourages good rhythm. Tee five balls in a row a few inches apart, as shown. Then hit all five without stopping, swinging and then stepping forward to hit the next ball.

(*Tony Roberts*)

3.

Two-Shaft Drill

This drill is designed to help keep your clubshaft on plane on the backswing and forward swing. Line up two shafts down your target line with the ball in between. Swing back (1) and down (2). At these positions the clubshaft should be pointing at the rear shaft on the ground. Swing through (3), at which point the clubshaft should be pointing at the forward shaft on the ground.

(*Tony Roberts*)

1.

2.

Over the Top Drill

From the top, swing the club to the outside and down across the ball the outside the target line to inside. This drill is useful for retraining a swing that comes too much from the inside. It's a practice swing you see Corey Pavin make on the golf course.
(*Tony Roberts*)

4.

112

3.

5.

6.

1.

2.

1.

2.

3.

4.

Pump Drill *(left)*

Take the club to the top (1), then halfway down (2), back to the top (3), and halfway down again (4). This teaches you to delay the early uncocking of your hands. (*Tony Roberts*)

3.

Split-Grip Drill

This drill does several things. Split your hands apart 3 or 4 inches, then swing halfway back and halfway through. It enhances the feeling of how your right hand and arm are farther away from you and down the shaft when you swing halfway back. At that point your right arm is above your left arm rather than folded to the inside, which improves your extension. The drill again keeps your right arm on top when you swing through and helps you to release the club instead of blocking it. (*Tony Roberts*)

115

Right Arm Only
with a Step

This is the same as the
Step drill but with just
the right arm. It again
teaches sequence of
motion and encourages
the feeling of the right
arm swinging freely
away from your body.
The right arm forms an
L at the top of the
backswing. Then comes
the step and the
"throw"—the swinging of
the right arm through
the ball. (*Tony Roberts*)

1.

2.

5.

116

3.

4.

6.

1.

2.

Step Drill

This teaches the correct sequence of motion, rhythm, timing, and balance, with the club falling and reacting to the shift and turn of the body. With your feet close together (1), swing back and turn, and just before you reach the top, step with your left foot (2). Then turn and swing through to the finish (3).

(*Tony Roberts*)

3.

1.

2.

3.

Left Arm Only

This is to train the left arm. Simply swing the club back and through with the left arm, coordinating the swing with the movements of the body. You also can hit balls this way.

(*Tony Roberts*)

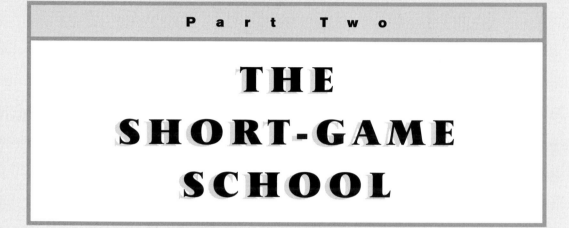

Part Two

THE SHORT-GAME SCHOOL

Let me put the short game in perspective. As I said earlier in this book, it is just 25 percent of the overall game. As I see it, the great players who have lasted over the years have always been good ball-strikers. There are a lot of great short-game players who never had a sniff of playing the Tour. There are a lot of good putters at clubs who have trouble winning the second-flight championship.

Having said that, I am by no means diminishing the importance of either putting or the short game. In fact, we put a huge significance into short-game practice at all of our schools. All the great ball-strikers who do well on Tour are also wonderful around and on the greens. And if making it on Tour is not your goal, which it probably isn't, putting, chipping, and the rest of the short game are where you can most quickly improve your score by developing some good techniques with good practice habits. You may never have the physical ability to hit a 275-yard drive, but you can develop the ability to get the ball up and down consistently from 50 yards in. For all players, but especially most amateurs, this is a tremendously important part of golf.

Having a great short game actually can make you a better long-game player, because it takes a lot of the pressure off. Plus, if you learn the proper technique, it will definitely improve your full swing. It also allows you to play more aggressively into the green, because you're not afraid of missing the green. Tom Kite once said, "Harvey Penick always wanted us to be good bunker players so we wouldn't be afraid to fire at a flag tucked next to one."

I've spent a tremendous amount of time with Jackie Burke, the former PGA and Masters champion and winner of fifteen other tournaments on the PGA Tour. I've played many rounds with Jackie, and he has conducted numerous golf schools with me. He's a great teacher of all aspects of the game, and he's particularly expert in the short game. He has worked extensively with players like Miller Barber, Steve Elkington, Phil Mickelson, Hal Sutton, and many others. As I've mentioned, he feels that golf is a game of targets, and he points out that everyone knows targets are missed. He beat this into my head and into the heads of all the players on the University of Houston team.

Each year Jackie would invite the top players on that team to practice and play at Champions in Houston, the course that he and Jimmy Demaret built. There we learned from him the importance of getting the ball up and down, being able to save par after a bad drive or a bad approach. It's unlikely that anyone can be on his or her game for three or four days in a row. In a tournament situation, whether it's the U.S. Open or your club championship, your ball-striking is probably going to be a little off in at least one of your rounds. You still need to shoot a decent score to stay in contention, and that's where the short game comes in. As a drill, I have some of my better students try to break 80 while missing all eighteen greens in regulation on purpose. When you can do that, the fear of shooting a high round in competition tends to disappear.

Saving strokes around the green early in a round often gives you a bonus—you get back on track mentally and you start hitting your full shots better. It usually works that way.

Also—and this is what is really important about the short game—the short chipping and pitching strokes incorporate all the components that are important in the full swing. In making the short shots, you bring into play movement of the body, path of the clubhead, angle of attack, angle of the clubface at and after impact, contact, left wrist and left forearm position at impact, and the relationship between the clubhead, hands, and body through the hitting area—all similar, if not identical, to what you do in the full swing. So by practicing and improving your short game, you will start to hit your long shots more solidly and consistently, because the fundamentals you're learning will work their way into your long game as well.

I mentioned earlier that hitting a long tee shot is the fun of the game. Well, working on your short game not only will help you become good around the greens, which immediately translates into lower scores, it also will help you hit more of those long drives that are so enjoyable.

For that reason, I'd encourage you to practice this 25 percent of the game a lot more than that. Spend at least 50 percent of your time practicing chipping and pitching. And as you become more proficient at the long game, spend even more time on the short shots. Chances are you'll continue to show improvement in both areas.

Putting

Putting is an art. There is a theory, widely accepted in the game's teaching culture, that putting is 43 percent of the game, or some such number. That's because putts allegedly make up that percentage of the average number of strokes per round. Well, I completely disagree with the theory. A good portion of those putts are tap-ins or very short, almost unmissable strokes. In most golf matches around the world, those are called gimmies—they are not even putted. Putting in our total teaching concept is just part of the overall short game, which is given 25 percent of the total weight.

Again, however, that doesn't diminish its importance, especially for the amateur. The putt is the last stroke on every hole, every round, every tournament. You may do everything else well, but if you can't make putts, you can't play. Conversely, good putting can make up for a lot of sins committed in getting from tee to green.

Golf is a mysterious game, as anyone who has played it can tell you. But one thing is certain: when the golf god wanted to share his secrets on putting, he had a direct line to Jackie Burke, who I believe has no equal in this area. Burke's ideas have shaped my theories of putting. Jack Nicklaus credits Burke with giving him his entire putting concept. Ben Crenshaw, who is a legendary putter, says Burke's advice was instrumental in developing his ability on the green.

Even though putting is the shortest stroke, the list of fundamentals or commandments is quite long—but that's a paradox in keeping with golf's mysterious nature. So from my time with Jackie Burke, Gary Player, Carl Welty, Paul Rungum, plus observing players like Jack Nicklaus, Ben Crenshaw, Brad Faxon and Tom Kite, here are my ideas on putting.

THE TEN COMMANDMENTS OF PUTTING

Commandment 1: Never consider putting a science.

Putting is an art form. Trying to be perfect leads to overtrying and overanalyzing. It makes you rigid and mechanical. That's not what great putters do.

Commandment 2: Know what good putters have in common.

- They have a routine.
- They read greens expertly—slope, lay of the ground, grass type, grain, wind, location of water. They walk around the line, because this enables them to feel the incline of a slope and notice subtle undulations. Being a good "green reader" is far underrated.
- Good putters bend low to the ground, especially near the cup.
- They know that the slower a ball is moving, the more the break or slope in the green affects it, and they know that the middle of the hole is the entry point on the line along which the ball is breaking.

- They know that speed is everything, especially with longer putts. One great Burke tip is, On very long putts, to walk halfway to the hole and double that distance to calculate speed.

- They face the hole and look at the line with both eyes open. As they look at the hole, they make an effort to relax their bodies.

- They walk the line of a putt in rhythm—not too fast or too slow, and not too rigidly. This rhythmic but concentrated gait enables the player to build a proper stroke pace.

- They relish the moment when it's their turn to putt. They execute their routine with supreme confidence. The green is their stage, and like great actors, they love the attention. They take charge and enjoy the applause. Bad putters do just the opposite. They look scared and they have awful body language—all of which, by the way, matters a whole bunch.

Commandment 3: Breathe smoothly and take one or two long breaths.

In Japan, these are known as *zazen* breaths. Inhale through the nose and exhale through the mouth. Breath control calms the nerves and fosters greater concentration. On makeable putts, your mind, not technique, is your greatest asset; see the line and see the ball rolling in at perfect speed, all before you hit the putt. This is what separates great putters from everyone else. When the mind fixes on the read, the putter, the golfer, the ball, and the hole are all one, and a precise stroke happens naturally. This may sound illogical, but forget logic. This is golf. To that end, Nicklaus says, "When I want to hit the ball a long way into a headwind, I swing slower and easier."

Commandment 4: While breathing and concentrating, don't forget the key fundamentals of the stroke.

In other words, if you're in a storm at sea, say your prayers but don't take your hands off the oars. The fundamentals:

- A simple stroke is best—one in which the blade remains relatively low to the ground and square to the target line; one that allows center contact every time; one that encourages correct feel and feedback over and over; one that with practice becomes natural and automatic, a stroke that repeats.

- On our scale of one to ten, most golfers would do well to have their grip pressure at three or below.

- Use one arm or the other as the dominant force. Burke encouraged a right-hander to feel the stroke in the right fingers, hand, and forearm, seeing the right arm as a piston. This is exactly what Nicklaus does. Some golfers will putt better by focusing on the left arm, wrist, and shoulder. One-sided putting simplifies things—it allows the mind to focus.

- A good tip is to feel the stroke in the center of your back. The end of the fulcrum is the pivot point of the stroke.

- The hands do very little, and the end of the grip does not travel a great distance—the less it travels, the better. This is a tremendous piece of advice. Read this tip five extra times!

- On long putts, you should stand tall and take a slightly open stance, for two reasons: you'll see the line to the hole better, and your arms will swing more freely toward the target.

- The length of the stroke must be long enough to have good pace.
- It is not necessary to go back and through the same length. That's hogwash, unless of course it happens to work well for you.

Commandment 5: Take a long-term positive approach to improving your putting.

If you have a bad putting round—and who hasn't?—don't dwell on it. Instead, dismiss it, tell as few people as possible, and turn your attention elsewhere. One bad putting round does not a bad putter make. When you putt well, short of committing the sin of pride, shout about it from the rooftops. A positive attitude is essential on the putting green, because nothing breeds success like success. Others will start to think, "Wow, that player always makes the key putts!" That's the best feedback you could ever hope for.

Commandment 6: Golf is a game, not work.

When you practice, entertain yourself. Make your practice fun by playing games or contests.

Commandment 7: Practice only as long as you can concentrate.

Stop when you're not having fun or if you lose focus. Short, focused practice sessions are often the most productive.

Commandment 8: Forget Commandment 7 if you are going to have to become a great putter to make a living.

Then practice till the cows come home. Build up your ability to concentrate until you get "it"—the magic! Then revert back to Commandment 7.

Commandment 9: Experiment with the following:

- To get their balance, many great players pick up their toes and/or heels as they get set to putt.

- Some believe that positioning the weight forward (toward the hole) makes for a more level stroke.

- Try positioning the arms and hands beneath the shoulders—this may help you relax.

- Some greats, like Crenshaw and Justin Leonard, have found that aligning their eyes inside the line improves their accuracy. It encourages an inside-to-down-the-line stroke, considered by many to be the most natural. Another name for it is open-to-closed.

- If you feel comfortable with an open-to-closed stroke, then follow your inclinations. In the end, any stroke that repeats has the potential of becoming a great stroke—or, as the great teacher Percy Boomer said, of "becoming fixed in those grooves or channels of your mind."

- Practice direction only under correct conditions— indoors on a putting track or a good putting rug or in the corner of a putting green where few people have walked. Don't overpractice short putts or directional control on a putting green. Traffic patterns around the hole can prevent a person from receiving accurate feedback. Lumps, bumps, foot impressions, spike marks—these imperfections sometimes impede rather than enhance performance. Occasionally you find unmakeable putts. Incorrect feedback might prevent you from reaching your putting goals. If you practice short putts on a green, try picking a position far from where the holes are cut and putt to a tee.

- If you are not a good short putter,

  Practice putting on a chalk line or between two clubs.

  Practice your stroke without a ball . . . a lot!

  Putt on a track that is built to force you to fix your stroke.

  Videotape your stroke.

  Putt with your eyes closed.

  Try cross-handed, split-grip, reverse-split, or claw grip.

  Put a dot on a ball and watch it during your stroke.

  Putt sidesaddle.

  Putt left-handed.

  Close your left eye.

  Look at the hole as you make your stroke.

  Try the long putter—it encourages a pure pendulum action.

Commandment 10: Thou shalt not exceed thirty-six putts per round.

Ever. Count all three-putts as whiffs. It's like adding a stroke to your score for no reason at all.

Given those commandments, there are some basics to look at in putting. As with the full swing, all can be modified to an individual's choice, as long as they work to get the ball in the hole.

THE GRIP

The purpose of the putting grip is to stabilize the hands and prevent excess hinging at the wrists. Unlike in the full swing, you don't need great speed in the putting stroke, so the less hinging you have, especially on short putts, is usually better.

The so-called standard putting grip is the reverse overlap. This is

Putting Grip

The common reverse overlap putting grip is formed by laying the club across the palm of the left hand, with the handle running diagonally from the base of the forefinger along the heel pad or the lifeline between the heel and thumb pads (1). The V formed by the thumb and forefinger of the left hand points to the left shoulder (2). All four fingers and the thumb of the right hand go on the handle, the V pointing to the right shoulder (3). The forefinger of the left hand overlaps the fingers of the right (4).

(*Tony Roberts*)

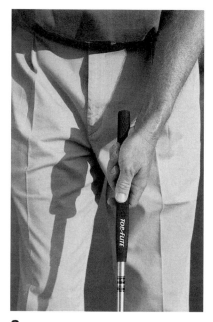

1.

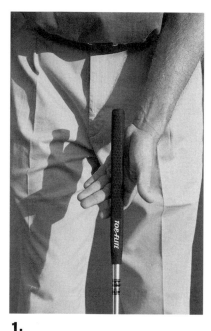

2.

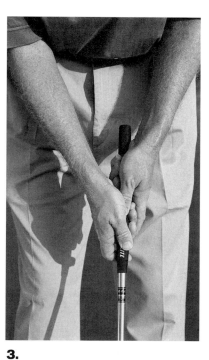

3.

4.

formed by laying the club across the palm of the left hand, with the handle running diagonally from the bottom joint of the forefinger across the heel pad or even against the lifeline between the pads. All four fingers and the thumb of the right hand go on the handle, and the forefinger of the left hand overlaps the fingers of the left. Position the hands on the club so the V formed by the thumb and forefinger of the left hand points to the left shoulder and that same V on the right hand points to the right shoulder. This in effect puts the two hands in opposition and restricts excessive hinging at the wrists. It also helps eliminate twisting of the putter blade. It helps the face stay square longer.

A variation of that grip is the double-reverse overlap. The positioning of the two hands is the same, but the little finger of the right hand overlaps the middle finger of the left, and the left forefinger overlaps only the first three fingers of the right. This grip places the hands closer together on the putter handle and tends to make them work more as one unit.

You can use whatever grip you want, as long as it's effective in stabilizing the hands. The so-called ten-finger grip or your regular full-swing grip are options.

THE STANCE

The position of your feet can be pretty much anything you want it to be—wide, narrow, open, or square. Many great putters stand open to the ball—Jack Nicklaus comes quickly to mind—because they can see the line better from that position. But others place their feet square to the line. I don't normally recommend that your stance be closed, because that tends to obscure your view of the line and gets you aiming too far to the right. However, if you see better from a closed stance, stick with it. The key here is to be comfortable and relaxed, and to see the line.

The putting setup,

down the line.

(*Tony Roberts*)

THE POSTURE

Again, the operative words are comfort and relaxation. Many good putters bend low from the hips, especially on the shorter putts. Nicklaus, maybe the greatest short putter ever, is once more a good example. Yet Raymond Floyd went to a longer-than-normal putter so he could stand more upright and save his ailing back while practicing, and he's one of the best putters ever. Crenshaw stands relatively erect on all putts.

How the arms hang seems to make little difference. Crenshaw lets his arms hang straight down, with no bend at the elbows. Nicklaus's elbows

No

An incorrect putting setup, with the hands behind the ball.

(*Tony Roberts*)

The putting setup, face-on. (*Tony Roberts*)

are both bent. It's a matter of preference and, of course, how low you bend to the ball.

Most good putters have the shoulders square to slightly open. Again, closed is not recommended.

Too much tension can be a killer in putting. My first teacher Al Mengert gave me a great visual that can help. Stand up to the ball without a putter and let yourself go limp, as if you're a balloon that's just been deflated. The air goes out and you just slump over, free of tension, your arms hanging.

Then have somebody put a putter in your hands. Learn this tension-free feeling on the practice green so you can duplicate it on the course. Keep your grip pressure at about three. It's okay to experiment with different grip pressures. The late Jerry Barber, a world-class putter, held the putter very firmly. Yet most other top putters hold the putter lightly.

And do not form a tripod! By that I simply mean that you should not push down on the putter when you address the ball, thus transforming your two legs and the putter into a tripod. If you do, you will feel that you can't take the putter away smoothly, and you'll tend to jerk it away, often to the outside. So ground the club very lightly when you address your putt.

 THE EYES

Your eyes ideally should be aligned parallel to your target line. In other words, your head should be square. Theoretically, your eyes should be set directly over the target line, although most good putters have them a little inside. Remember, I said golf is a mysterious game. A few players—Scott Hoch is one—even set the eyes outside the line. You should be aware that if you do this, you'll tend to take your stroke outside as well, and that's okay if you can compensate. But I don't recommend this setup. Eyes over the line or slightly inside works best. Adjust your distance to the golf ball until you are comfortable.

 THE STROKE

I recommend a pendulum-type stroke, which is a little different from the all-arms stroke you see a lot of people make. I like to feel that the two arms and the shoulders form a triangle, and that that triangle stays intact back and through. As Commandment 4 holds, I find it better if you feel that one hand

1.

2.

The putting stroke
is like a pendulum,
back and through
(*Tony Roberts*)

3.

4.

135

1.

2.

The putter swings slightly
inside, back to square, and
slightly inside again, the face
remaining square to the arc.
(*Tony Roberts*)

3.

4.

and arm has more control than the other. But one super tip is to feel as if you're rocking your shoulders, or even that you're making the stroke with the muscles in your upper back. Your shoulders act as a teeter-totter. That keeps the triangle solidly intact and prevents the grip end from moving too far, which is what we want. It makes the stroke as simple and repetitive as possible.

I suppose in a perfect world your putterface ideally would remain square throughout the stroke. However, keep in mind that this is square to the arc of your stroke and not necessarily to the target line. It might be straight back and straight through on a very short putt, but as the stroke gets longer, the putterhead will start moving to the inside and the face will appear to open. Then, as you swing it back into the ball, it might come back to the target line and appear to close. Then the opposite happens on the follow-through, the putterhead swinging back off the line. This path will tend to become more pronounced the more your eyes are set inside the target line. This is natural, just as in the full swing, so don't fight it. For all but the short putts, you can't swing any club like a Ferris wheel.

Make your stroke as rhythmic as possible. It's okay to have the length of the backstroke and the follow-through should be approximately the same. However, especially on short putts, if you build any kind of tendency into your swing, it should be to make the follow-through shorter than the back-swing, just the opposite of what most believe. A short and slow backswing with a lot of follow-through is a combination that usually doesn't work too well. It actually leads to deceleration and poor distance control. It's better to develop a "hit and hold" sensation. That encourages acceleration. Gary Player, Brad Faxon, and Ben Crenshaw have always had a very distinctive hit with a hold. The next time you watch a Tour tournament on television, you'll see a lot of that. You won't see any kind of hit and drift through the follow-through. It's almost like a gymnast who nails a landing. She sticks it and poses for the judges. It's the same with putting—hit and hold. Sometimes you'll almost see a rebound—Faxon is a good example, and he may be the best putter out there right now.

A good way to practice this is to stick two tees in the green, not as far apart as the length of your putterface, and put the ball down just behind them. Then stroke and hit the tees for resistance, stopping at this point. You'll soon develop the feeling you want.

Once you have decided on the line of your putt and are set up to it with the blade properly aligned, think distance, not direction. Speed control is critical, especially on the longer putts. It's a matter of practicing enough to develop an instinct for the length of stroke you want to make, how hard you want to hit any given putt. Phil Mickelson, another great putter, has a trick on long putts that you might find helpful. He takes one practice stroke that he knows will be too short, then another that he knows will be too long. Then he tries to find the middle ground and goes ahead and hits the putt with that stroke. He triangulates the distance like an army captain zeroing in on the enemy.

Speed control, along with accuracy, goes out the window if you don't make solid contact every time. This is essential to good putting. You must contact the middle of the ball with the middle of the club. Most of today's putters are perimeter-weighted, which reduces the twisting of the putterhead when you strike the ball off the center of the face. But it doesn't eliminate that twisting. An off-center hit alters the speed at which the ball will roll. This affects your distance control, of course, and also your accuracy, because the ball usually won't hold the line you've picked out to the hole.

Nolan Henke, a very good putter on the PGA Tour, once told me that striking the ball with the center of the putterface and rolling the ball smoothly was basically all he tried to do. He felt that his face could be as much as five degrees off on a short putt and he'd still make it every time with a good stroke and a solid hit. I was very impressed with that line of thinking.

So work on solid contact. You can use training putters with prongs, or put imprint tapes on the putterface, or simply put some powder on the face so you can tell where you're striking the ball. We recommend that most students at our schools use a putter with a line on it. Of course, check that line to make sure it is located on the sweet spot.

George Archer, another of history's great putters, once said that using a perimeter-weighted putter was fine, but eventually he would get sloppy and would have to go back to working with a blade that wasn't as forgiving to get better feedback on off-center hits and regain his precise feel for striking the ball on the sweet spot. That's a pretty good tip.

The best stroke and the solidest contact in the world aren't going to help you a lot if you can't read greens. This becomes simply a matter of practice and experience, and I'm sure it's not taught enough. You must learn how to judge the side-to-side breaks in a green as well as the effect of uphill and downhill slopes. This involves being familiar with different grasses and with grain, which is the direction in which the grass is growing. Grain plays a particularly significant part on coarser, usually longer Bermuda greens. The grass almost always grows toward the setting sun, toward nearby water, or away from nearby mountains. A good way to tell is to examine the cup. Remember, all greens have some grain. If one side of the cup is brown, with the dirt exposed, the grain is running in that direction. It's sometimes hard to tell early in the morning when the cups are freshly cut, but it always shows up later in the day. On close-cropped bent-grass greens, grain is usually not as much of a factor. Check to see the sheen of the grass on bent greens. Shiny means it's down-grain. Dark means it's into the grain.

On your home course, you eventually memorize the breaks, and you don't have to work very hard at reading the greens. But when you travel and play new courses, green-reading becomes critical. Tour players stand out from amateurs in their ability to read greens, because they're playing different courses all the time.

Here's a clue that is very simple, yet works for about 80 percent of your putts. An architect is going to do two things when he builds a green. First he has to drain the water off the green. Then, in most cases, he must make the green somewhat receptive to a shot. That means that in most cases the green will slope from back to front toward the fairway. It may be subtle, but the slope will be there. On a very short hole, or on a reachable par 5, he might make the hole a little tougher by sloping the green in the opposite direction, but usually it will go from back to front.

That means that in most cases, if you are to the left of the hole, the putt will break from left to right. If you are to the right of the hole, it will break from right to left. If you are short of the hole, it will be an uphill putt. If you are past the hole, it will be a downhill putt. You still have to factor in the humps and bumps and tiers, but whenever you're in doubt, go with this simple McLean rule. Trust me, it works.

When reading a green, remember that a wet putting surface will have an effect on the way the ball rolls. The simple strategy here is to allow for about half as much break as under dry conditions.

To finish this section on putting, let me pass along another bit of putting wisdom from Jackie Burke. You may be thinking, "This putt is going in." Or you may be thinking, "This putt isn't going in." Which thought is wrong? They both may be. According to Burke, either one is an example of poor concentration, and he is adamant about it. He says you must be focused on the basics while you are putting, and thinking about the results of the putt is not the way to do it. He says that once the ball is struck, there is nothing you can do. The ball is on its way. It could hit a depression or a spike mark. It might break opposite to the way you expected. Or it might go in. Thinking about these things causes anxiety and a focus on results. Jackie says to forget results. They will come from proper execution. Execute your best stroke.

You do have the power to control the execution of your stroke, or what is directly in front of you—the putter and the ball. Anticipating results and worrying about them gets your concentration over at the hole and not directly out in front of you where it should be. Worry about results and you are likely to forget all about your execution. Simply take care of your putting stroke. Execute your fundamentals, and you will get results.

That applies not only to putting but to literally everything else in your life.

HOMEWORK DRILLS FOR PUTTING

Right Hand Only

This will train your right hand and arm to work properly in the stroke. (*Tony Roberts*)

Left Hand Only

This teaches you the motion of the left hand and arm.

(*Tony Roberts*)

Putt to a Can *(left top)*
Practice putting to a soda can
sitting on the green. When
you become proficient at this,
putting to the hole will look a
lot easier, because the hole is
much bigger. (*Tony Roberts*)

Two-Board Drill
(left) • Lay a couple of
two-by-fours on the green,
just slightly farther apart than
the length of your putterhead.
Practice making short pendulum strokes without hitting
the boards. (*Tony Roberts*)

Flagstick Drill *(far
right)* • Lay a flagstick on
the green and practice making strokes back and forth on
top of it. This will tell you if
the putter is going too far
outside or inside the line.
(*Tony Roberts*)

142

The chip shot is used from just off the green when you want to carry the ball over intervening grass and land it on the green. The distance from which you can use the chipping stroke varies according to the distance to the hole and how much putting surface there is between the edge of the green and the cup.

The rule here is "minimum air time, maximum ground time." And let me give you a piece of advice. If you can putt, putt. If the ground between you and the edge of the green is relatively smooth, don't be afraid to take out your putter. Your worst putt will usually be better than your worst chip.

The chip is simply an extension of the putt, with certain modifications. We teach many of our students to use the putting grip in chipping. However, your stance should be narrow, and approximately 70 percent of your weight should be on your left side, so the stance is different. Position the ball slightly back in your stance and close to your body. Your eyes should be almost over the ball, just as in a putt. Arch your wrists a bit, which puts the handle up so the shaft of the club is more upright. This minimizes wrist and body movement. It also helps get the heel of the club off the ground, which helps going through to the ball because of less resistance with the grass. Your hands should be slightly ahead of the ball at address, and they stay ahead throughout the stroke. Feel that either your left hand or your right hand is dominant, just like in putting. Then just go ahead and make the simple stroke I have described. You want to hit the ball first, so take the club up slightly on the backswing and make a slight downward brush coming through. Keep the grip ahead of the clubhead and the left wrist solid through the shot. Never, ever do you want the clubhead to pass the hands before impact.

That's why in chipping you want your grip pressure a little tighter,

1.

2.

The chip is just a
long putt, with
wrists firm and
weight on the left
side. (*Tony Roberts*)

3.

4.

not lighter. You want it up around six or seven, because you don't want the wrists activated. You need resistance for the short chip shot. It's a must.

After you strike the ball, allow your eyes to follow the ball. Don't freeze your head. On longer chips, there will be some footwork and your hips will move slightly with the stroke.

Finally, I hate to see the left arm pull too much past the ball. This drag, block action is unnatural and looks very rigid. It also doesn't work very well. Instead, keep the grip end of the club just off the left thigh as you finish the stroke.

THE THREE-CLUB SYSTEM

For effective chipping from different distances, I suggest a three-club system and the use of ratios—the difference between how far the ball travels in the air and how far it rolls on the ground. At our golf schools we recommend using a seven-iron for long chips with a one-quarter-to-three-quarter ratio. Obviously, we adjust the formula for faster or slower conditions, but it's a solid system. The ball travels a quarter of the distance to the hole in the air and rolls the remaining three quarters. For shorter chips, I suggest an eight-iron with a one-third-to-two-thirds ratio. That means one third in the air, two thirds on the ground. When you don't have as much green to work with and need more loft and control, I recommend a pitching wedge and a fifty-fifty ratio. If you have a favorite chipping club and want to use it all or most of the time, I have no problem with that. But you need to establish an accurate ratio with that club. I find the three-club system to be much easier and more versatile. It covers all the basic chips.

Learn to judge your distance and these ratios accurately. In practice, pace off different distances. Learn exactly how far one quarter and one third and one half are on any given length of shot. If you do this enough, you'll be able to judge the distances on the course much more accurately. Even during a round, pace off your distances, if you can do so without holding up play.

Having established these ratios, now all you have to worry about is the landing area. Focus on where you want the ball to land. I recommend you chip to a circle and not an exact spot. I envision a 6-foot circle which if I calculate correctly leaves me margin for error and a putt inside of 3 feet. The rest will take care of itself. Of course, you have to take into consideration the speed of the green and whether your chip is uphill or downhill. Sometimes these factors will change the ratio and hence the speed of your stroke for any given club. Usually you can accommodate this simply by changing clubs and applying the appropriate ratio.

Once you develop a reasonable feel for distances and ratios, the chip becomes just a long putt. That simplifies this part of the game, and that's what we're after.

Pitching

JUST A SMALLER GOLF SWING

If hitting good pitch shots is a mystery to you—and it is to many amateurs— just bear in mind that the pitch is just a small swing, with certain adjustments. That should simplify the process for you. It is also one of, if not the most important, shots to learn. We believe a good pitch swing is almost a lost art.

The pitch is a shot with more air time and less ground time. It's used in a situation where you can't chip or putt. For example, when you have to go over a bunker to an elevated green with the flag tucked close to the edge, you're going to have to pitch the ball. Depending on the amount of height you need on the shot, you can use a nine-iron, a pitching wedge, a sand wedge, or a lob wedge, if you have one.

The basic pitching swing, with hands swinging back to nine o'clock and through to three o'clock

(*Tony Roberts*)

1.

2.

3.

4.

Set up for a pitch shot with a relatively narrow stance. Your feet should be slightly open, with your left or front foot pulled back from the target line a little more than the right. But keep your shoulders fairly square or parallel to the target line. Too many people set up far left, which causes a cutting action on all shots.

In the standard pitch, it's critical to understand that you have to strike the ball first, then the ground. That's what gets the ball in the air. Many amateurs think that to get the ball in the air with a pitching club they have to lift it. This comes from a golfer's beginning days when the most important objective was to get the ball in the air. What happens then is the club comes in on an arc that's too shallow, and you either hit the ball in the equator and top it or hit the ground behind it at the bottom of your arc. One of our Master Instructors, John Mills, has been particularly helpful to all of our instructors in emphasizing the importance of teaching this shot properly. As John says, it's almost a lost art. Almost nobody coming to our schools can make a decent pitching stroke. Sadly, the basic pitch stroke is fundamental to having a good full swing. Apparently, this shot is given little attention by teachers and students alike!

The club must come into the ball on a descending path, making a descending blow. It must not be a flippy-wristed shot where the left wrist is bent at impact. The clubhead hits the ball, then pinches the turf in front of the ball. The ball gets collected in the grooves of the club and spins backward, and that's what gets it into the air.

To encourage this descending blow, set your weight 60 to 70 percent on your left side at address and keep it there during the swing. Shift your weight minimally, if at all, during the backswing. At address, your hands should be ahead of the ball, and they should return to this position at impact. You need an early wrist cock on the backswing. You must get the club up in the air so it can come down on the ball. This really surprises many of our students who are trying to stiff-wrist these shots. A terrible mistake. Feel that you are hinging the club with your hands. If you have trouble with this, lay

1.

2.

3.

4.

To learn to make an
early wrist cock on the
backswing, lay a two-
by-four 12 inches
behind the ball, and
don't hit it while you are
swinging back and
through. (*Tony Roberts*)

a two-by-four on the ground about 12 inches behind the ball and make sure you don't hit it going back or coming down.

Through impact and beyond, the left wrist should be flat. That keeps unwanted hand action out of the swing, but remember that there is hand action in pitching. Strike the ball and clip the grass in front of it. Your divot should start not behind the ball, nor where the ball was but just in front of or on the target side of the ball. (If you are taking deep divots as you strike the ball, your swing arc is too steep or you are playing the ball too far back in your stance.)

Although there is no weight shift on the backswing, the body definitely turns and shifts as you swing through impact and into your follow-through. Think about keeping the clubshaft centered on your body through impact and at the finish. Don't pull the club past the ball with an extended left arm. One shot we teach has your belly and the club pointed straight at the target when you finish. On higher shots, the wrists rehinge and the club points at the sky. Your weight should be on your left leg, just as with the full swing, and there should be some air under your right heel. Your right knee will move forward, which helps tremendously with your shot feel. Practice holding that finish position so the feeling becomes ingrained.

For a small pitch, you want a high backswing and a low follow-through, not the opposite. Sometimes I think we are the only school in America teaching this method. That is frustrating because I know it is the correct technique. This action will produce a nice crisp hit and a stop. The great short-game instructor Johnny Revolta always said, "Hit and resist." Swing the club down through the ball and then resist at the finish. Keep the left wrist flat, especially on the shorter shots.

Our key words for the pitch were developed by Master Instructor John Mills: hinge, turn, and hold. Remember those three words. Hinge the club on the backswing, turn through the shot, and then resist. Keep the left wrist flat at impact and the left hand ahead of the right. Keep the body turning through the shot. Feel that your right hip or your right pocket is turning

Finish the pitch shot with the club and
your belly pointing at the target.

(*Tony Roberts*)

No

Trying to lift the ball with the club
and falling back with the body is a
sure way to ruin the shot.

(*Tony Roberts*)

past the ball. Hit the ball and then the ground. Finish with your belly and
the club pointing at the target. That's solid pitching technique. It helps
everybody!

About that ball position: I'm now seeing most amateurs play the ball
too far back in the stance. It should actually be about in the middle. But
remember, it changes from shot to shot, depending on lie, slope, wind, and
club selection. To determine that, set up to the ball with your feet together,
then spread your feet, moving both of them the same distance. The ball will

then be positioned where you want it for a standard pitch. Keep in mind that variations are allowed. If you want the ball to fly lower and bounce and roll farther before checking up, play it further back in your stance. If you want it to fly higher and land softly—the so-called lob or flop shot—play it a little farther forward. You'll have to experiment to find out which ball positions produce which kinds of shots. I think it's ridiculous for amateurs to attempt to play all shots around the green back off the right toe or even behind the toe. That's Pitching 101—beginners only.

That said, to learn the feeling of the descending blow you need in pitching, practice hitting low punch shots. Play the ball slightly farther back in your stance, and make sure your hands are well ahead of the clubhead com-

For the high pitch or lob shot, position the ball slightly more forward in your stance and swing the club up on the follow-through. (*Tony Roberts*)

1.

2.

3.

1.

2.

To pitch the ball low, position it
back in your stance, about off the
right toe, and finish with the club
lower and extending toward the
target. (*Tony Roberts*)

3.

153

ing into impact. This encourages the crisp contact you want with all pitches. It will also give you the feel needed for solid iron shots, perhaps for the first time in your life.

It's especially important in pitching to keep the club on a good back-swing plane. To check this, lay a club on the ground off your back toe, parallel to the target line. When your club is parallel to the ground on the backswing, it should be directly above and in line with that club on the ground. (Again, this pitching drill will help your full swing technique.)

Because you will face a lot of different situations and distances in pitching, you can't have just one swing. You have to learn to make the club move farther, but you also have to learn to make it move faster and slower. So I'm going to give you four basic swing lengths—a one-quarter swing, a half swing, a three-quarter swing, and a full swing. Picture yourself standing inside a clock. The ball is at six o'clock. For the one-quarter swing, your hands swing back to eight o'clock and through to four o'clock. For the half swing, they go back to nine and through to three. For the three-quarter swing, it's ten to two. For the full swing, it's back to eleven and through to one. No uneven swings, no eight-to-three or nine-to-one swings. Your follow-through should match your backswing at each length, just as a pendulum swings.

Remember, I'm talking about the hands at these positions, not the clubhead. This is where keeping the left wrist flat and not breaking down comes into play. If you can visualize a clock, with your hands swinging through to four o'clock, the club should still be pointing downward. At three o'clock the club should be parallel to the ground. At two o'clock the club will be pointing upward, and at one it will be up and pointing behind you. That's why you want to practice holding your finish, so you can monitor the position of your club.

Don't worry about any in-between positions. Practice those shots and learn how far the ball goes with each at normal swing speed. So if you have to hit the ball only 5 yards, you'll have to make a nice slow swing. You do that by turning your body more slowly. You have a speedometer right in your belt buckle. You make the ball go faster or slower by the speed with which you turn your body.

Understand that the speed of the swing, no matter how long or short, will affect the flight of the ball. This is good to remember, for example, when you must make a high, soft lob shot to a close pin. Watch Phil Mickelson sometime. He's a master at these shots. He makes a longer swing than the shot would normally call for, but it's always a slow swing.

Shaft Drill

To check your backswing plane on the pitch shot, lay a shaft on the ground off your back toe, parallel to the target line. Check to make sure that when your club is parallel to the ground on the backswing, it is directly above and in line with that shaft (1), neither inside it (2) nor outside it (3). (*Tony Roberts*)

Golf
School

1. Yes

2. No

3. No

THE FOUR PITCHING DEATH MOVES

There are four "death moves," any one of which can keep you from becoming a good pitcher of the ball:

- No wrist hinge on the backswing
- A short backswing and a long follow-through, which almost always indicates that you're trying to help the ball up
- A breakdown of the left wrist through impact, which may be the deadliest sin of all
- A weight shift onto the right leg on the backswing, which almost always will cause you to hit the ground behind the ball.

Avoid these mistakes at all costs. Practice executing the fundamentals correctly and the death moves will go away—or never appear. Remember: hinge, turn, hold.

Bunker Play

USE THE BOUNCE IN THE SAND

The concept of teaching bunker play that we use in our schools is not one that I invented on my own. The concept comes from three great teachers—first Johnny Revolta, then Claude Harmon, then Ken Venturi. The latter two, I think, got a lot of their ideas from Revolta, one of the renowned short-game teachers of all time. Harmon, the 1948 Masters champion and long-time professional at Winged Foot and Seminole, was a wonderful teacher of all aspects of the game, but he was a wizard at playing and teaching the bunker shots. Venturi is one of the best bunker players and teachers I have ever seen.

I also got a lot of good information from Gardner Dickinson, who worked a lot with Harmon at Seminole, and from Jackie Burke, who also worked for Harmon when he worked for Claude at Winged Foot. One winter I worked at Marco Island in Florida and played quite a bit of golf with Gene Sarazen, who invented the sand wedge and obviously knew how to use it.

So what I'm about to tell you, and what I hope you are about to learn, comes from some of the greatest bunker players and teachers in history. Absorb the concepts and practice them, and you'll never again have to worry about playing successfully out of sand.

Open the club so the flange or bottom rides first through the sand.
(Tony Roberts)

157

Many, if not most, higher-handicap amateurs tremble at the thought of landing in a bunker. That's mainly because they have no idea how to play out of sand. The good player, in contrast, would much rather be in the sand than in greenside rough. It's a much easier shot. It's hard to convince most amateurs of that, but it's true. If you learn the proper techniques, most sand shots are among the easiest in golf. On the other hand, without good technique, the bunker shot is truly a shot to be feared.

The key to successful sand play is to use the bottom or sole or flange of the club (all those terms mean the same thing), and not the leading edge. The sand wedge has what we call "bounce" built into the design. That means that the trailing or back edge of the club is lower than the leading or front when the club is soled on the ground. Depending on the design, most iron clubs have some amount of bounce, maybe 1 or 2 degrees. The sand wedge has a lot more than that, usually 10 or 12 degrees. Using this bounce correctly allows the club to skid through the sand under the ball and lift the ball out on a pile of sand. If you strike the sand behind the ball with the leading edge of the club instead, you will invariably leave the ball short of its target, probably still in the sand.

 THREE DEATH MOVES IN THE SAND

At our golf schools, I insist our students learn the three "death moves" for sand play—three things you don't want to do in the sand. Understand these and you will never fear the sand again.

- Grip the club tightly with tension in your arms and hands
- Play the ball back in your stance or have your hands ahead of the club so you catch the sand with the leading edge
- Take a short, low, or flat backswing.

Let's look at how to avoid these moves and do the sand shot correctly. Just by avoiding these three major errors, you will greatly improve your bunker game.

Take a slightly open stance, your weight a little on your left side, about 60 percent. Work your feet into the sand so you're firmly anchored and also so you can feel the texture of the sand. Slide your hips a bit forward toward the target. It puts a higher percentage of your weight on your left leg, and makes it easier to play the ball forward in your stance. Position the ball slightly forward of center. Never put the ball behind the center of your stance or lean your hands forward. That's bad news. You can open the clubface in two ways—by leaning the shaft away from the target (hands back) or by fanning the clubface into open position. Never put your hands ahead of the ball or close the clubface.

Relax and let your arms hang limp. Use a light grip pressure, maybe a two or three for the normal bunker shot. If there is any shot in golf where tension kills you, it's in the bunker. Julius Boros was one of the best bunker players in the history of the game. He would just amble to the ball, set up casually, and take a lazy swing. For anyone that ever saw Julius, this is a great image. That's the kind of swing that works in the sand. Quick swings with tension don't. So feel lazy and relaxed when you're making your swing.

Make a minimal weight shift on the backswing and let the club travel up with a free cocking of the wrists. Make a good shoulder turn with a long, relaxed swing. That shoulder turn is crucial to building easy speed and often our students don't make a good turn. Remember, low and short doesn't get it. One of the principal things you have to feel is getting the club up on the backswing. Harmon would use a simple little drill with his students. He would set a rake at a 45-degree angle behind them, on their swing line. He wouldn't allow them to hit the rake on the backswing, which would force them to swing the club up the way he wanted.

Now you have to get the club down and through the ball. The motion is the same as for the lob shot—keep the club in front of your body

1.

2.

3.

Using a lazy swing, strike the sand behind the ball and let the flange skid through the sand under the ball to lift it out. (*Tony Roberts*)

1.

2.

3.

4.

5.

6.

4.

5.

6.

as you turn through, and finish facing the target. The only difference is that now you want to strike the ground—in this case the sand—first instead of striking the ball. A good thought is to throw a cushion of sand out of the bunker and let the ball go with it. Hear the slap as the bottom of the club strikes the sand and the bounce lets it ride through. Trust the fact that as the club skids through the sand (under the ball) and throws out that cushion, the ball will come out with it.

Harmon always encouraged a right-arm release on this shot, and so do we. In the bunker, the clubhead actually gets out in front of the hands as it passes under the ball and continues through. You don't want any pulling on a bunker shot. You want a release. So don't be afraid to let that right arm go. Let it swing.

How far behind the ball should the club slap into the sand? Here my system varies greatly from many others. We don't teach trying to hit 1 or 2 inches behind the ball. In practice, draw two lines in the sand, about 10 inches apart. Make a few swings and see where your club is hitting the sand. I need to see any student I teach make seven or eight swings in a row where they can land between those two lines. If they can do that, I can guarantee success. When you set up correctly and the club gets cocked up properly in your backswing, you can hit from 1 to 6 inches behind the ball and still get excellent results. That's the great thing about the method, and that's what makes bunker play a lot easier than most golfers think. You don't have to be as precise as you are on grass. Just look at and aim for a general area, allow the clubhead to pass underneath the ball, and exit on the other side.

The perfect distance to hit behind the ball is actually 3 to 4 inches. This is a great revelation to most golfers. Experiment to see what works best for the particular consistency of sand in your bunkers, or on any course you happen to be playing. That's why a few practice bunker shots before you play a strange course is a good idea.

If you're going to make an error in the sand, make it too far behind the ball rather than too close. That's another reason why our system is so good. If you hit too far behind, you'll leave it in the sand or on the bank of the bunker, and it costs you one stroke. Conversely if you get too close and hit the ball first, you can just put an X on the scorecard, because you're going to hit it into a lake or a tree or bury it in the top of the bunker over the green. Your return shot often leads to absolutely no shot. Harmon used to call it the home run ball—he hated the sound of club-ball contact and considered it the worst death move you could make. Never hit the ball first!

In hard or wet sand, you obviously have to make some adjustments. You don't want to use the bounce of the club as much, because it will tend to skid into the ball, so square the face at address. If you have a 60-degree wedge, use it instead, but it doesn't have as much bounce on it. Or you might want to use your pitching wedge and cut through the sand with the leading edge, especially in wet sand. The ball will come out faster from firm or wet sand, so allow for that in the force of your swing by slowing down.

You will encounter some unusual shots and lies. Here's how to deal with them.

THE SHORT BUNKER SHOT

To hit the short bunker shot, when the flagstick is close to your side of the green, you do just the opposite of what you might expect. You don't regulate the distance by the length of your backswing. You regulate it by the length of your follow-through. Again, this is a big surprise to our students. Make a full backswing, but instead of releasing the club as you do for a normal sand shot, make a short finish and hang on or block it—hold the face open as you finish. That makes the ball go shorter and land softly. What you don't want to do is take a little-bitty backswing and hit through the shot, because that greatly increases the chances of skulling the ball or leaving it in the bunker.

I've worked very hard on this shot with tour pros like Tom Kite, Brad Faxon, Christie Kerr, and Lenny Mattiace. This past year Lenny finished number two on the PGA Tour in bunker saves. We had worked particularly hard on the short bunker shot prior to the season and it paid off, big time.

THE LONG BUNKER SHOT

This is one of the hardest shots in golf. To play it, square the face, again position the ball a little forward in your stance, then swing almost as if you are hitting a three-wood. Don't get the club quite so elevated on the back-swing—it's more like a normal swing, because you want to take a shallower cut of sand. And the important thing is to accelerate through impact and all the way to the finish. Also, you have to hit closer to the ball, about an inch behind it. Because of the distance required, you don't have that big margin of area behind the ball. It's the one shot where I advise you to focus precisely on the spot where you want the club to enter the sand.

We also teach people to use a seven- or eight-iron for long bunker shots. This can be very effective and is not tremendously difficult to learn. Simply open the clubface and follow the rules I've outlined. The ball will come out lower, but will carry farther. With a little practice, it can be a great weapon.

Last, to avoid long bunker shots, I tell our students to be better course managers. By that, I mean don't give yourself the opportunity for long bunker shots. For example, don't smash a three-wood into the front bunker and then notice the pin is at the very back of the green. If your best shot can't easily carry a bunker, lay up with an iron. Avoid the superlong bunker shot whenever possible. Even a tour player hates this shot.

1.

2.

For the long bunker shot, square the face, make a more normal swing, and strike the sand closer to the ball. (*Tony Roberts*)

3.

4.

SLOPING LIE BUNKER SHOTS

From uphill and downhill lies in the bunker, simply align your shoulders as much as possible with the slope, then swing with the slope. From a downhill lie, be very sure to get the club chasing down the slope, through the sand, and under the ball. Keep in mind that the shot from the uphill slope will go higher and shorter and stop quickly, while the downhill shot will come out lower and run a long way.

If the ball is on a slope above your feet, your swing will be flatter and come around more and the ball will come out to the left, so adjust your aim accordingly. If the ball is below your feet, just the opposite applies—your swing will be more upright than normal and the ball will come out to the right, and it will also go a shorter distance, so aim more left than you normally would and give it a little more speed.

For the downhill bunker shot, align your shoulders down the slope and make sure the club chases down the slope through the sand.
(*Tony Roberts*)

1.

2.

1.

2.

For the uphill bunker shot, align your shoulders up the slope and swing the club up the slope line through the sand. (*Tony Roberts*)

3.

4.

167

BURIED LIE BUNKER SHOTS

There are three basic types of buried lies—the fried egg, the plugged lie, and the partially plugged lie. It's important for you to be able to identify each, because the techniques for playing them are slightly different. We teach our students to understand that all buried lies are not equal.

The fried egg lie is one in which the ball is sitting down in the center of a crater of sand. It usually occurs when the sand is soft and dry. The plugged lie is one in which the ball is buried halfway or more in the sand, with little or no crater around it. The partially plugged lie is one in which the ball is less than half-buried in the sand with little or no crater around it. To be really great at these shots, the golfer must adjust to all types of buried lie variations. That skill only comes from experience and practice.

In general, shots from these lies are played in just the opposite fashion from a normal bunker shot. You take your sand wedge, or even a pitching wedge, square the face, and hood the club. You set most of your weight on your left side. You put the ball back in your stance, not forward. You put your hands forward, not even with or behind the ball. You grip the club tightly, not lightly. And instead of releasing through the shot, you strike down sharply behind the ball and bury the club in the sand. It's just the opposite of the standard bunker shot technique I teach.

Squaring and hooding the clubface turns the club into a digger, which is what you want. You have to get the club under the ball. So set up the way I described, take the club back and down steeply and slam the leading edge into the sand behind the ball.

With the fried egg lie, you have to strike the sand on the edge of the crater. Because that's usually quite a ways behind the ball, much more force is required to get the club under the ball and you must make a very steep, descending blow.

With the normal plugged lie, the same technique is used, but you

These are the
three types of
buried lies: the
partially plugged
lie (1), the plugged
lie (2), and the
fried egg (3).
(Tony Roberts)

1.　　**2.**　　**3.**

enter the sand only about an inch behind the ball. The ball will come out much easier, so you won't need nearly as much force in your swing.

The partially plugged ball will come out more easily yet, so use the same technique but with less force.

In all these cases, from a flat lie, the ball will come out low, with little or no spin, and will run a long way, so allow for that if possible.

If you are a more advanced player, you can play the partially plugged lie with the ball more forward in your stance and an open clubface. You will need a very steep angle of attack, but the ball will come out more softly and higher. Practice the shot, however, before you try it on the course.

Many Tour players these days are playing all buried lies with an open clubface. They just take the club up steeply and pound down on the sand with enough force to get under the ball, letting the force of the sand lift the ball out higher and more softly. But this requires talent and strength—and practice. The open-faced technique works much better with an uphill buried lie. With a downhill buried lie, don't try it at all.

To be a good player, it's important to be adept at the sand game, so spend a lot of time in the practice bunker. Then, as Tom Kite says, you can fire at those tucked flags and not worry about wasting strokes recovering.

HOMEWORK DRILLS FOR BUNKER PLAY

If you have a buried or fried egg lie, swing the club up sharply and strike down with a steeply descending blow behind the ball or at the edge of the crater. (*Tony Roberts*)

1.

2.

3.

Swing Up a Rake

To practice a steeper backswing for the sand shot, have somebody hold a rake behind the ball at a 45-degree angle and swing up along that line. (*Tony Roberts*)

1.

2.

Ball Off Board

To get the feeling of the flange riding through the sand under the ball, put a board in the sand, heap a pile of sand atop it, and slap the flange against the board, letting it skid and lifting the ball out on the pile of sand. (*Tony Roberts*)

1.

2.

Lines in the Sand

Draw two lines in the sand about 10 inches apart, put the ball in the middle, and swing through those lines to get the ball out. That shows you how much margin of error you have to make an acceptable sand shot. Try this drill with the right arm only to get a feel for the correct right-arm action in the shot. (*Tony Roberts*)

171

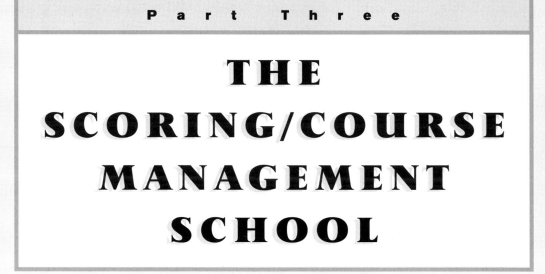

Part Three

THE SCORING/COURSE MANAGEMENT SCHOOL

Shooting low scores involves a lot more than simply swinging correctly and hitting solid shots. Many amateurs believe the one secret to shooting low scores is mastering the elements of a good swing. This is, of course, a misapprehension. To quote my friend and fellow teacher Butch Harmon, Tiger Woods's coach, "The art of scoring is not about playing swing, it's about playing golf." Butch and I have done a lot of golf schools together, and I couldn't agree more with that statement.

To play good golf and enjoy the game even more than you do already, you must learn to set up to the ball correctly and employ a technically sound, rhythmic swinging action, one that performs virtually on automatic pilot and repeats itself under pressure. You must also be able to hit a variety of shots from on and off the fairway. Of course, these on-course assets are not all that you need to get the ball in the hole in the least number of shots and finish the job, as the legendary Bobby Jones used to say. Unless you learn to manage your game sensibly and smartly, and on a steady basis, you will do yourself a disservice. In short, you will be blocked from shooting the lowest score you are capable of shooting, and as a result you will fail to lower your handicap, which is every golfer's dream.

If you follow the game faithfully, watching the pros play golf on television or at a tournament course, you know that some players find their way to the winner's circle after seventy-two holes, even though they hit the ball far less perfectly than some of their competitors. These players cash in because they think intelligently out on the course, carefully plan each shot to the best of their ability, and eliminate mistakes.

I tell students that they too can beat the course if they learn to think strategically. When you do that—and it is an art—you virtually ensure a score of par, birdie, or bogey and greatly reduce the chance of recording a double bogey, triple bogey, or the big X.

Gary Player, Dave Stockton, and Hale Irwin are three senior players who have won major championships on long tough courses even though they are not long off the tee. Of the LPGA players, veterans Juli Inkster and Betsy King do not hit the ball nearly as long as Laura Davies or Annika Sorenstam, yet they are still winning tour events. Justin Leonard stands out among PGA Tour players as being one of the smartest strategists. Granted, since switching to metal-headed clubs, Leonard has hit the ball longer than ever before, but by no means can he be considered a power hitter. All the same, he is very successful on tour because he has an exceptionally good golfing head. He proved what a smart golfer he is by winning the 1997 British Open at Scotland's Royal Troon links and finishing second to Davis Love in the PGA Championship, played that year on the very long and demanding Winged Foot golf course in Mamaroneck, New York.

What do these players and other top pros and amateurs do that sets them apart? That is the $64,000 question. And the answer is not what you expect—that they simply hit fairways and greens.

Players who are supreme, clear-thinking strategists—and Jack Nicklaus is probably the premier player in this category—do a variety of special things that take place from tee to green. Before providing you with specific strategic tips for saving shots without changing your swing, let me give you some general insight into how the game's best players think strategically and what is taught at our schools.

Preround Strategy

Know where you are going. First and foremost, expert players are well aware of the hole's shape when standing on the tee. They are also aware of treacherous rough or hazards bordering the fairway or green, severe slopes in the fairway, wind direction, precise distances to ideal landing areas, the position of the flagstick, the hardness of the entranceway to the green, and the speed of the putting surface. One chief reason low-scoring pros and amateurs know the course is that before a tournament starts, they carefully study all aspects of the course. Usually they will draw a diagram of each hole on a memo pad, designating where and where not to hit the ball and noting exact measurements to good and bad areas. Also, the player plays at least one practice round before the event, so he or she can add important notes to the hole schematics and confirm or change yardage.

Interestingly, very often the player will walk from the green toward the tee, hoping to notice new things when seeing the hole from a different perspective. It's surprising what you can see from this angle, and I don't just mean a better way to play the hole. You'll probably see some subtle slopes in the green that previously went undetected. You may see that a water hazard cuts deeper into the fairway than you figured. You may see a new bunker or tree that you didn't even notice by the corner of a dogleg, or you may notice that the tee points off to the right, into the woods. For these reasons, our instructors teach the same strategic advice when playing Doral, PGA West, or Grand Traverse during a school. We encourage our more serious students to take the time to walk the course at home and to carry a pad, so that like the pros, they can keep a visual record of each hole and refer to it out on the course during competitive or noncompetitive play. If you want to make a serious effort to improve your scores, you should look at a golf course, particularly the one you play on most of the time, as your opponent. In the same way that a boxer or football player looks at films to size up his opponent, you should size up the course by doing the walk-backwards exercise and writing things down about each hole on a pad.

If this preround strategy seems like a lot of work, remember the words of the old Chinese proverb: "Every journey starts with one small step." If you don't take that first step and do everything in your power to prepare for your battle with the course, you can expect more than your share of mistakes during every round you play.

Don't Automatically Grab the Driver

Pros and top-notch amateur golfers know that a driver is not always the automatic choice of club from the tee on a par 4 or par 5 hole. However, high handicappers make the mistake of taking the driver out of their bag practically every time, mainly because they count on making their best swing. I advise you not to make the same mistake. You will run the risk of hitting the ball through a dogleg or into a pond, deep rough, or trees, or hitting into an out-of-bounds area that may well be within your range. Let's not forget, too, that if you know in your heart that hazards lurk and you really shouldn't be hitting a driver, you may find yourself steering the ball.

Learn from the top players, who play golf for a living. The next time you arrive on the tee, take a good look at the hole, particularly if you are playing it for the first time. If you don't have a caddie, which will probably be the case, study the map of the hole that usually is featured on the scorecard. Take the following things into consideration: the distance of the hole, the approximate distance to fairway bunkers and other trouble spots, the distance to the corner of the dogleg, the distance to the last flat area of fairway before a severe slope, and wind conditions. Once you factor in all these variables, honestly determine if you would be better off hitting a three-wood or a long iron rather than the driver. Remember the old golf adage "It's not how, it's how many." Play the best shot for you. Some days that play is safer than other days. Always play the percentages.

Hit to a Specific Line

Another thing good golfers concentrate on is hitting the ball on a specific line. I've already gone into the fine points of aim and alignment. However, I would now like to give you some added visual tips for hitting the ball on target.

When we take students out onto a tee to prepare them to swing, we tell them to imagine a big window or a doorway several yards in front of the ball and directly in line with the target. Either of these images will intensify and narrow your focus. Further, this imagery will help you block out any hazards, thereby allowing you to concentrate on hitting the ball specifically at your target (whether that target is a point located in the left center of the fairway, its center portion, or an area on the right side of the fairway). Many top players use these visual tips.

Another tip, designed to help prevent steering or guiding the club through impact, is one Gary Player uses. He images a brightly colored ribbon suspended horizontally a short distance in front of him and running between two poles at chest height. Player tries to break through that imaginary ribbon on the downswing. This mental trick promotes added clubhead acceleration in the hitting area and ensures a full finish.

Tee the Ball Carefully

Experienced players are very careful to set the tee in the ground the same way every time. Normally, with a driver, they want at least half of the ball to be higher than the top edge of the clubface, since this position encourages a clean and solid upswing hit through impact. However, some players take this to the extreme, teeing the ball extra high. Other players, most notably Scott Hoch, tee the ball fairly low, with the top of the clubface practically even with the top of the ball, to promote an upright rather than an overly flat swing, plus a power-fade shot.

On par 3 holes, be very specific about the way you tee up the ball when hitting different irons. When preparing to hit a short or medium iron, tee the ball just above the grass or one-quarter inch high. For long iron tee shots, tee the ball slightly higher. At our schools, we teach students to tee the ball up on short holes (rather than hit the ball off the turf), because having the ball on a tee promotes confidence and makes the shot easier to hit. However, the beauty of our teaching philosophy is that we like to offer players options, based on what works for the game's best players. Speaking of options, numerous professionals promote low, driving shots by tipping the tee slightly forward. To promote a higher, softer-landing shot, tip the tee back slightly. In reading about these nuances, I'd like you to feel free to experiment. But once you find a tee strategy that works well, stick to it.

Tips for Par-Three Strategy

While on the subject of playing par 3s, I want to discuss some information that we give our students to help them improve their score on these kinds of holes.

SELECTING THE RIGHT CLUB

To select the correct club, when the tee markers are well behind or ahead of a yardage plate in the ground (or a signpost designating the hole's distance), do not simply guess how much space there is between the two. Pace off the number of yards, then add or subtract that yardage from the yardage shown on the tee marker or sign you used as your reference. Do not automatically trust the yardage on the scorecard. The distance from where the hole was measured to where the tee markers are placed can be quite a difference. Many golfers ignore this important fact.

When caught between two clubs, most players will benefit by choosing the stronger club. We like to see our students do the same thing. However, if on average you perform better and do not steer the swing when you are more aggressive, go with the weaker club. Tom Watson is one of those players who prefers to take the weaker of the two clubs and swing harder.

Ernie Els and Steve Elkington are two players who tend almost always to lean toward the stronger club and the smoother swing. That's what I almost always recommend.

KNOW WHERE THE PIN IS

Make sure you know where the pin is. Is it located dead in the middle of the green? If not, how far back is it, or how far forward is it? You can determine the answers to these questions by asking your caddie, looking at a sheet that shows the day's pin placements, or seeing whether a little flag or ball attached to the flagstick is located at its top, in the middle, or near the bottom. These markers on the flagstick designate the back of the green, the middle of the green, and the front of the green, in that order. Some greens are very long from front to back, so if you fail to figure the pin placement correctly, you'll likely hit the ball well short or well long of the hole. For example, the seventeenth green at Doral's Blue Monster course is 56 yards long. Consequently, there could be a four-club difference between hitting a shot to the front or the back pin. Depending on where the pin is, I normally advise different strategies. For example, if the pin is cut on the back of a two-tier green, I recommend that you take the stronger of the two clubs you are considering, because if you hit the shot too far, it will just run over the back of the green, where no sand bunkers or hazards normally exist. If you hit the shot just right or even a trifle weak, the ball will still probably reach the top tier, where you will leave yourself a birdie putt.

GAUGE THE WIND

Be sure to gauge the wind too, by looking at the movement of the flag and noting in what direction branches on the top of trees surrounding the green and near the tee are blowing. Alternatively, determine wind direction by tossing some grass into the air while standing on the tee and seeing how it's affected. Generally, we advise students to take one more club for every ten miles per hour of headwind, one less club for every ten miles per hour of following wind. Average players should aim farther left when playing into a left-to-right crosswind, farther right when playing a shot into a wind blowing from the opposite direction. Good players who have the ability to work the ball should play a draw into a left-to-right crosswind and a fade into a right-to-left wind. A very good final tip is to check the wind at the clubhouse prior to teeing off. Most have flags around the clubhouse that will give you a good indication of wind direction. Note this, because on the golf course, the wind may swirl and mislead you.

LEAVE YOUR EGO IN THE BAG

Always play your game and avoid letting your ego stand in your way. Do not ever try to hit an iron on a par 3 just because your playing partners did. The smart strategy is not to worry whether you are the only one in your group who needs to hit a metal-wood. If that's the club that will allow you to reach the pin, play it.

PLAY YOUR NATURAL SHOT

Many of our students look at me or my fellow instructors in amazement when the question of placing shots comes up. Because a larger number of middle- and high-handicap players lack the ability to hit good shots consistently where they want to, they figure there is little point in listening to a lecture on ball-placement strategy from the tee. They figure only pros, who can hit pinpoint shots hole after hole, are interested in this subject. Well, as I tell all my students—men, women, juniors, and seniors—"Listen up." Just because you lack a pro's talent to hit dead-straight shots, fades that fly from left to right, or draws that fly from right to left, I know you hit one basic shot most of the time. Even if that shot is a slice or a winding draw, there is usually a shot pattern you can rely on. Forget trying to do everything perfectly and hit the straight shot, which even Ben Hogan called "the hardest shot in golf."

Time and time again during a playing lesson, I see students hit the ball out of bounds or into trouble simply because they failed to set the ball down on the correct side of the tee and allow for the curvature of their personal shot. For example, I'll see a slicer tee his ball on the left side of the tee box, then hit a drive that starts left and never gets a chance to move right, back to the center of the fairway. The ball makes contact with the branch of a tree and falls straight down, into more trouble. In most cases, you can easily avoid this score-wrecking shot if you tee the ball up on the side of the teeing area that will best accommodate your shape of shot. In this case, to allow for the fade or even a pull slice, you should tee up on the far right side of the tee, or at least in the middle of the tee box, depending on how much your shot usually curves. The more it curves, the farther on the right side of the teeing area you should tee up your ball. Those of you whose natural shot is a big draw should set the tee down on the left side of the tee and aim down the right side. But in planning your strategy for either a slice or a draw, don't aim too far down one side. A good rule is to never aim where a dead-straight shot will kill you.

KNOW YOUR DISTANCE WITH EACH CLUB

Fine players also know precisely how far they carry shots hit with every club in their bag. This is why they rarely get caught hitting a drive in a fairway bunker at the corner of a dogleg. It's also why they rarely dump shots into water hazards fronting the green on par 3 holes. I teach all my students to hit practice shots to specific targets and to note carefully how far they hit each club. That way, they know how far they carry the ball with different clubs. At Doral, La Quinta, Grand Traverse, and my other schools, we also advise students to hit shots in varying wind conditions, so they learn to factor this variable into their strategy when playing a hole.

Pick Your Spots and Shape Your Shots

At our players' schools, we help golfers take their game to an even higher level. Much of our work comes on the golf course. Surprisingly, many amateurs just get up and hit the ball, rather than using their talents to their advantage. What we do instead is encourage them to shape shots off the tee so they use the whole fairway. That means playing an intentional draw or fade. Ideally, when adopting this shot-making strategy, you put the ball in the best position to set up an attacking approach to the flag.

During a playing lesson, we show our students where they lose shots by letting their machismo or ego get out of hand. Often we advise them not to shoot at the hole even after playing the perfect drive. I'm a big believer in aiming at the dead center of the green. I want them to avoid a nearby water hazard, a dangerous slope that could cause the ball to bound into deep green-side rough, or a yawning trap filled with soft sand that could lead to a difficult buried lie. The simple advice of forgetting the pin and aiming to the center of the green could be the best advice you'll ever hear. These same basic principles apply to Tour players, but since they can hit a variety of shots expertly, they can afford to take more chances and flirt with trouble when their game is on, in order to attack a tight pin.

Rest assured, when a pro arrives at her ball in the fairway and prepares to hit an approach, she is considering a lot more than just the distance to the flag, which is all many amateurs do. No pro or fine player shoots a good round without thinking strategically. There are times when a pro even thinks it is smarter to miss a green and land the ball in a spot where she can pitch or chip from. I know this surprises you, so let me cite an example of how this strategy could come into play.

Let's say a pro faces a shot from 190 yards to a lightning-fast two-tier green featuring a very steep incline from its lower level to its top level. Let's assume that the pin is cut on the lower level and there is no trouble in front of the green. The trouble, a very big, deep bunker, sits behind the green. For the sake of this example, assume too that the pro hits a four-iron an average of 190 yards and his five-iron an average of 180 yards. Well, in this situation, many players would simply pull out the four-iron and swing away. Smart pros know better. They realize that if they hit the four-iron extra flush, the ball will probably fly up to 200 yards and finish on the top tier, leaving them in a very difficult two-putt position and with almost no chance for birdie. What they do instead is hit the five-iron slightly harder than normal to propel the ball farther than their typical shot with that club. If the shot doesn't quite come off as planned, they leave the ball short of the green, where they can easily score par, and maybe birdie, by hitting a chip or pitch to the pin on the lower level of the green. If they do hit the shot as planned, there is a good chance that the ball will fly 185 yards, land on the front portion of the green, and stop quickly, leaving the player with a fairly short birdie putt—over flat ground, to boot. Now the pro can make an aggressive birdie attempt. By the way, the chip shot from in front of most greens is generally one of the easier shots in golf.

Believe it or not, top players understand their own game so well and have it down to such a science that they usually figure out where the best spot to land the ball is if the shot fails to come off as planned. We call these "exit areas." For example, in hitting a shot to a pin cut behind a bunker on the right side of the green, they may figure it is best to play a fade rather than a draw. If they start the shot well left of the flag and it fails to fade, the ball will land in the fat of the green, where they still have a reasonable chance of scoring birdie. (If you plan to hit a draw and don't catch the ball solidly, it will probably land in the bunker. Also, hitting a draw to a close pin could easily cause the ball to land a little hot and finish in deep rough behind the green, where it is very difficult to hit a soft chip next to the hole.) If you do play a draw, simply aim for the center of the green. This is not a green light pin location for you.

Even the pros fail to play perfect shots all the time, although one would not think so, considering the large number of hours they devote to practice and how good-looking their swings are. Most do, however, turn in low scores at the end of the day. Those who break par are the ones who know how to get the ball in the hole—the ones who are more concerned with the ins and outs of shooting a low score than with judging how pretty their swing is. Learn from this. Before you make a swing, look carefully at all of the obstacles in front of you and take the time to think out where you want to hit the ball, no matter what type of shot you face—short, long, easy, or difficult. Like a good chess or billiards player, think a step ahead, so you avoid putting yourself behind the eight ball.

Be Careful with Overconfidence

One thing that makes this game so crazy is that when you are playing well, you often think you can hit any shot in the book. You are superconfident and seemingly in control of your emotions. During these times, you feel as if your game is on automatic pilot. Strangely enough, this is when you have to be extra careful, because you are vulnerable to overconfidence. A little voice of temptation in your head sways you to attempt a low-percentage shot. It's easy to succumb, particularly if you believe that hitting the shot well could set you up to do something miraculous, such as eagle a par 5 hole. If this profile doesn't match yours, I ask you to beware, because sooner or later you will get into a course situation that causes you to read a yellow- or red-light situation as a green-light one.

As talented as Curtis Strange was during his heyday, he found out how instincts and the temptation to be heroic can take over and cause you to hit the wrong shot at the right time. In the 1985 Masters he had a chance to win late in the fourth round, after making a fantastic comeback from an opening 80. On that fourth day, he took the lead going into the thirteenth hole, a par 5, where he hit a solid drive. Now he faced a big decision: to lay up in front of Rae's Creek, the water hazard fronting the green, or to go for the green in two. Curtis is one of the smartest strategists ever. You don't win two U.S. Open Championships without being a great thinker. However, on this day he was too anxious to wear the prestigious green jacket given to winners of this coveted championship. So he let his emotions and ego get away from him. Instead of laying up and taking his chances to get up and down with a wedge and a putt for birdie, he gambled. Plunk! Yes, Curtis dumped the ball into the water and made bogey. Nevertheless, he was still very much in the championship coming to the fifteenth hole, another par 5, also with water in front of the green. Once again Curtis hit an excellent drive. Once again, however, he gambled and lost. There was to be no green jacket for Curtis.

The lesson I want you to learn from this story is that even though you sometimes feel pumped up, don't risk going for broke if it is going to take your very best shot to put yourself in the ideal scoring position. Look for alternative ways to play the hole. If Curtis had laid up on both par 5 holes, he would probably have scored at least one birdie and flown home to Virginia with the prestigious green jacket.

Measure Risk Against Reward

This may be the most important thing I can tell you about course management: weigh the risk versus the reward. It depends on your skill level, of course, but usually you'll find that the risk far outweighs the reward. If you are deep in the woods and have the option of threading a spectacular shot through the trees and maybe reaching the green or chipping out safely into the fairway, the chip-out is almost always the best course. And don't rush the recovery shot. Figure out where you want the ball to finish to set up the next shot. Then choose the club you know will propel the ball out of trouble and hit it the correct distance. If you have to hit absolutely your best shot with a three-wood to carry a water hazard and get to the green, laying up is almost always the wisest thing to do. And always check your lie, because it always dictates what you can do with the shot. If you have a poor lie in the fairway, or if your ball is buried in deep rough and Tiger Woods couldn't get it out and on the green, don't you try either.

In a bunker, when the ball is buried near the front wall, you rarely want to get cute. Aim away from the highest part of the lip and try to hit the ball to one side of the hole, thereby setting yourself up to save par or score no worse than bogey. Do not try to ram long putts into the hole on very fast, sloping greens, even if you are in desperate need of a birdie in a stroke-play competition. Instead, stay cool and feed the ball to the hole, so that if you miss to one side, you are left with an easy tap-in for par. We call these defensive putts. In our schools we simply teach our students to lag the ball to the hole in these situations, which often gives you the best chance of holing the putt.

If you absolutely have to gamble, if the circumstances of your match or the tournament demand that you play the boldest shot, if you have nothing to lose if you miss, go ahead. But those situations are rare. The great majority of the time, beware of low-percentage risk-taking. Think before you act—that is my message to those of you who want to keep the big score-wrecking numbers off your card. The key question I always ask my students is: "What am I trying to do?" Don't forget to ask and answer that question every time.

Your Routine Should Be Routine

Shots that count for your score are somehow always harder than shots on the practice tee, where if you miss you can simply rake over another ball and try again. So every shot you take on a golf course should be preceded by a routine that gets you ready to hit that shot comfortably. That preshot routine can be anything you want, but you should do the same thing every time and in the same amount of time. Let me outline the routine we advise, which is similar to that used by most good players.

Stand a few paces directly behind the ball. Make sure to relax your shoulders, arms, and hands. Look at your target as you visualize the shot you want to make. You're focusing, tuning in, picking an intermediate target, and keeping that visualization of the shot in your mind. Assume your grip with the club directly in front of your chest and in the air. Now, still relaxed, walk to the side of the ball, step in with both feet together, place the club behind the ball, and aim it down your target line. Now adjust your left foot and then your right so your stance and body parts are aligned properly. The time factor of my routine starts when I drop the feet into position. You might want to start yours when you start walking to the ball. In any event, do it the same way every time. For many golfers, the amount of time you take before you actually move into the hitting position is not all that important. You can take more or less time in this segment. However, once the feet are put into position I feel the clock is on, and taking the same amount of time from then until you swing is very important.

Once I'm set over the ball, I usually look once at the target as I waggle the club back and forth with my hands and arms, look back at the ball

1.

2.

Make your routine the same every time. My suggestion: assume your grip with the club in the air and your feet together (1); place the club behind the ball and aim it down your target line (2); adjust your left foot (3); adjust your right foot (4); look at the target and waggle (5 and 6); look back at the ball (7); look at the target again and waggle (8); look back at the ball (9); and go (10).

(*Tony Roberts*)

6.

7.

3.

4.

5.

8.

9.

10.

and then look at the target again, look back at the ball, and start my take-away with my forward press. That means simply two looks to the target, set, and go.

The majority of players on Tour look twice at the target and hit it. Some look once like Raymond Floyd, Lanny Wadkins, Tom Watson, and John Daly. Some, like Jack Nicklaus, look three or four times. I like two looks, but you do whatever you develop and feel comfortable with. Just don't spend too much time standing over the ball, which produces tension and allows too much time to think about mechanics and negative imagery.

Work on your routine in practice so it becomes habit, so you can perform it without having to think about it. The advantages to a pre-shot routine are undeniable, and we spend quite a bit of time rehearsing this at our three-day schools. You will definitely benefit by improving your routine, of that I'm sure.

Remember that the opposite of routine is random. Since most people want to be more consistent, having a pre-shot routine is a vital element to this goal.

I've given you a pretty good feel for the basics involved in playing the game strategically and intelligently. Now I will provide you with some quick tips that we give to students at our schools, mostly during playing lessons. Pay close attention and you will learn how to think your way to lower scores.

Good Strategy Starts on the Practice Tee

In warming up before a round, avoid just taking the driver out and beating balls. Instead, follow the same preround routine used by the top pros.

Begin your session with a few short wedge shots. Next, hit every odd club (that is, a nine-iron, a seven-iron, a five-iron, etc.), working your way to the driver. Hit only about a dozen drives, or else you will get tired or speed up your swing. Finish off your routine by hitting a few more half-shots with the sand wedge, as this will smooth out your rhythm and ready you for hitting a good drive off the first tee. I also like to finish off my practice session by visualizing the first hole I'll play, using my pre-shot routine, and hitting a good opening tee shot. After a satisfactory practice shot I go directly to the tee.

Get a Light Grip on Your Game

Just before the last round of the 1987 British Open, Jack Nicklaus told the leader, Greg Norman, to remember one thing: to relax his grip. This is a story I relate to all students, because this one tip does so much good for almost everyone. A lighter grip enhances your feel for the club, lets you make a less robotic swing, and encourages a free release of the club through the impact area. Remember our school mantra: Tension kills the golf swing!

Take the Club You Know Will Land the Ball in the Fairway

Some golfers who visit my schools are under the impression that it's better to hit the ball longer, even in the rough, simply because that leaves you a shorter approach shot into the green with a more lofted club. I disagree.

I prove my point by advising students to hit one ball from where they hit it in the rough and a second ball from the center of the fairway, 20 yards back. You'll soon see that short grass is better to hit out of than long grass, even if the shot to the green is longer.

Strategy on Doglegs

A hole that turns from right to left, or doglegs, is one that can be handled fairly easily by a low-handicap player, especially one who naturally draws the ball. Having said that, I see many natural power-fade hitters also hit the driver in this situation.

If you usually hit a fade off the tee, put the driver away. Instead, tee up a three-wood, which is much easier to draw. You can even toe the clubface in slightly. This strategy can put you in an excellent position to hit a short approach and make birdie.

High handicappers who normally slice the ball should never try this shot. If you fall into this category, aim at the left rough and let the ball drift back into the center or right-center portion of the fairway.

The same philosophy applies to holes that dogleg from left to right. These holes are easier for players who normally fade or even slice the ball. Just aim down the left side of the fairway and let it happen. Be aware, of course, that you need to reach the corner of the dogleg with your tee shot, so make sure that your normal drive is long enough to do that.

If you tend to draw the ball, aim down the right side and let the ball end up in the center of the fairway. Again, you must drive past the corner of the dogleg.

Another option is to turn your draw into a fade or at least a straight shot by opening the clubface a little and making a normal swing. Then aim down the left or left-center and let the ball wind up in the fairway with an unobstructed second shot to the green.

Strategy on Tight Holes

Hit your tee shots to the 150-yard marker on tight holes. When my students realize that the 150-yard marker can be reached with a two-, three-, or four-iron, many supertight holes become a lot easier for them to play.

The next time you face a tee shot on a tight hole bordered by deep trouble, pick out a club that will hit the ball to the scoring zones. On a 340-yard hole, for example, put the driver back in your bag and instead choose a club that will hit the ball 190 yards. That's all you need.

Read the Fairway Slopes

Most fairways, especially on modern courses, pitch and turn, sloping one way and the other. As you stand on the tee, or if you are planning to bounce a shot into the green, be aware of those slopes and how your ball will react when it lands. Often you will have to aim your shot down one side or the other if you want it to end up in the middle.

The Layup Shot

I have already discussed the wisdom of laying up. But do it correctly. Golfers who play at all levels really surprise me when it comes time during a round to lay up in front of a water hazard. Let's assume you have 170 yards to the water and you normally hit the five-iron that distance. Don't choose the five-iron and tell yourself that you will just ease up on the club. If you select that club, you will tend to hold back so much that you will probably decelerate through impact, leave the clubface open at impact, and hit a big slice or fat shot.

The best strategy in this situation is first to figure out the exact distance to the water. Next, plan on hitting an area of grass 10 to 20 yards in front of the water, depending on your skill level. I would rather see average golfers pick out an area of fairway farther back, then take a stronger club and make a free swing.

The other advantage of laying up well short of the hazard is that you eliminate the chance of having the ball hit a hard patch or a subtle downslope and bound forward into the water. And usually you want to lay up far enough from the green so you can make a full swing on your next shot rather than having to hit a delicate partial shot. The bottom line: be sensible, lay up short, and make a confident golf swing. The oldest rule in golf is "When laying up, lay up." We often repeat this rule since many golfers relax when laying up and actually hit their best shots. The shot goes much farther than expected and goes into the hazard. Never make this mistake.

On Iron Shots, Go Low When the Wind Is at Your Back

At one time in my golf career, I thought it was always best in this situation to hit the ball high and let the wind carry it. However, Ken Venturi helped me realize that any ball hit high with a strong wind behind your back cannot be controlled very well. So I now avoid the wind as much as possible by knocking the ball down with my irons. So should you.

When playing this kind of approach shot, say in the 120- to 160-yard range, use one higher club than normal and choke down on the grip slightly. You'll be surprised how much better you can control the ball.

The key during the swing is to deaden the action of the hands and wrists. Concentrate on the arms and shoulders, make a firm weight shift on the downswing, and finish low, as Venturi advocates. This technique produces a low punch shot that will stick when the ball hits the green. The wind won't be able to carry the ball too far or take off much spin.

Dealing with a Flyer Lie

If the ball lies in wet grass, or if moderately high grass behind the ball is leaning toward the target, the ball will usually fly much farther than normal.

That's because moisture or blades of grass fill the club's grooves at impact, lessening the backspin that will be imparted to the ball. You hit a sort of knuckleball shot, with the ball flying fast with little backspin.

To counter the flyer lie, I instruct medium- and high-handicap students to take a club that is at least one lower than usual. I tell better players to play their normal club for the appropriate distance but to counter the flyer effect by swinging on a slight out-to-in path and imparting soft cut-spin to the ball.

Examine the Texture of the Rough

It certainly is frustrating to find your ball in the rough after just missing a fairway. But bounces and bad lies are part of the game, and it is better to accept them.

I find when teaching at my schools around the country, that golfers automatically reach for a utility wood when the ball is in the rough. Normally this is a smart strategy, especially when the ball is sitting down. The new utility clubs feature a good amount of sole weight and also have cambered soles, design qualities that make it easier for players to recover. But you don't always need to reach for the lofted wood and run the risk of hitting an overly strong shot into trouble. During the summer months, the rough will often be burned out. In such circumstances, choose an iron that is right for the distance. The iron will have no trouble slicing through the dry rough. You don't have to worry about hitting a flyer over the green, since the moisture will have drained out of the blades of grass. Remember to carefully analyze your lie in the rough. Not all areas are equal in texture or depth. Make sure to always take a practice swing to feel the amount of resistance you will face. Also, grip firmer in deep rough as the clubface will tend to twist.

Faders: Think Before You Swing

In certain course situations, slicers often drop shots because they get too cute. For example, say the pin is cut on the far right side of the green, there is a creek to the right of the green, and the wind is blowing left to right. If you hit a natural slice, avoid starting the ball just left of the pin in an attempt to land a shot softly next to it, owing to the left-to-right shape of your shot and the wind. Aim to hit the area of fringe left of the green and let the wind blow it back to the middle of the green. If you hit your final target, you'll be in good shape to take your par and run to the next tee. If you go for the sucker pin and knock the ball in the water hazard, there is no telling what you will score on the hole, but it will probably start with an X.

Playing Par 5 Holes

If you are one of those golfers who stresses out the second you stand on the tee of a par 5 hole, mostly because you do not hit the ball very far, pretend that the hole is a par 6. This strategy will ease your mind and relax your body. As a result, you will generate much more clubhead speed and make a more fluid release through the ball without even thinking about it. You will probably have no problem getting near the green in three shots and still have an excellent chance to make a par. And if things fail to go exactly as planned, you will walk off the hole with a bogey 6, which is not a bad score.

Intelligent Wedge Play

A common problem among amateur players is hitting 75-yard wedge shots well short of the hole. This problem often occurs because the player chokes down on the club too much and makes too short and stiff a swing. For this shot, grip the club near the end of the shaft and make a fluid three-quarter swing. Remember to turn through the shot so that your belt buckle is facing the target.

Let Long Putts Die at the Hole

I know that you have probably read or heard it said that you will make more putts if you hit the ball hard enough to roll 17 inches by the hole. To me, this is a silly strategy, because it encourages you to knock the ball well by the hole. On long putts, simply try to get a feel for distance by eyeing the line from the ball to the cup. This is something I learned from our scoring specialist at PGA West, Dr. Craig Farnsworth, an eye specialist and expert short-game coach who teaches at our schools. This visual tracking process will help you gauge distance better and pace at such a perfect speed that the ball will die in the hole or come to rest close by the cup. Believe me, learning distance control takes a ton of stress out of the game. Save those superbold attempts for short uphill putts.

How to Enhance Your Direction Control on the Greens

In setting up to hit a putt, align the logo on the ball straight down the ball-hole line or along the line on which you want the ball to start. Brad Faxon is one golfer I've worked with for many years who employs this method. This strategy will give you added confidence and help you keep the clubface square throughout the stroke.

Special Shots

You will encounter many shots on the golf course that are different from the plain vanilla shots that you usually hit on the practice tee, so learn how to hit them. Find a way to practice these shots when it doesn't count, so you will be ready when it does. Make your practice sessions more fun by hitting all types of recovery shots including high and low hooks, and high and low fades to specific targets.

 ## SLOPING LIES

Unfortunately, not all your shots on the course are going to be off level lies. Hills are a fact of life in the game. So you must learn to play off uphill, down-hill, and sidehill slopes.

The shot from an uphill lie is usually the easiest for most players, because it's easier to swing up on the ball than down through it. On an uphill lie, align your shoulders and set your body with the slope. Your weight will favor your back foot as your body conforms to the slope. Play the ball forward in your stance, because the bottom of your swing will come later. Be sure to take at least one extra club, because the ball is going to fly higher and shorter than usual. The shot also will tend to go left, particularly from a severe uphill lie. In those cases, take two or three extra clubs and make a shorter, controlled swing. The shorter and easier the swing is, the lower the ball will fly.

From a downhill lie, which is the hardest shot for most amateurs, do just the opposite—align your body down the slope, with your right side higher and your weight favoring your front foot; play the ball back in your stance, and take a club with more loft. The ball will go lower and farther, and it could tail to the right. For this reason, favor the left side of your target area and open your stance slightly, which also helps get your left hip out of the way on the downswing. As with all unusual lies, swing within yourself,

1.

2.

Ball Above Feet

Your swing will be flatter, and the ball will tend to go left, so aim accordingly.

(*Tony Roberts*)

1.

2.

Uphill Shot

Align your shoulders up the slope and swing up.

(*Tony Roberts*)

Downhill Shot

Align your shoulders down
the slope and chase down the
slope with your club.
(*Tony Roberts*)

1.

2.

Ball Below Feet

Flex your knees more and
bend more from the hips. The
ball will tend to go right, so
aim to the left and swing
within yourself. (*Tony Roberts*)

1.

2.

maintain your balance, and strive for solid contact. A common mistake is not playing the ball far enough back in your stance. Be sure you don't do this.

On the side of a hill with the ball above your feet, be aware that you will tend to pull and hook the shot to your left. You can allow for that, playing out to the right and letting the ball come back to the target. Or, as I tell advanced players, you can fight it—take an extra club or two, open the face a little, and hang on more through impact with your left hand to keep the ball from going left. Whichever you do, grip down on the club a little and strive for balance throughout the swing.

The ball below your feet on a sidehill lie will tend to peel off to the right. This is a very difficult shot. You need to take a club with which you can make a comfortable swing. Make sure your weight doesn't get out on your toes. You need to flex your knees more and bend more from the hips. Aim fairly far to the left, allow for a loss of distance, and swing within yourself. If you swing too hard and get out of control, it's very easy to catch the heel of the club first and actually pull the ball to the left. Remember, always swing within yourself for this shot, or any severe sidehill lie.

FAIRWAY BUNKERS

The key to playing out of fairway bunkers, to achieve square contact and get the most distance possible out of your shot, is to keep your lower body quiet during the swing. Any violent action of the legs—or of the upper body, for that matter—will likely ruin the shot.

In the fairway bunker, the first rule is to take a club with enough loft to get over the lip in front of you. You might not be able to make it to the green, but at least you'll be playing your next shot out of the fairway and not from the sand again. If the bunker is flat and the lip is no problem, then choose a club or two longer than the distance calls for (I'll explain that in a moment).

1.

2.

The Fairway Bunker Shot

**Play the ball slightly forward of center (1); keep lower-body action to a
minimum (2).**

About 80 percent of your success in the fairway bunker is predicated
on the setup. Take a slightly wider stance than normal and work your feet
into the sand to stabilize yourself. Grip down on the club for better control
and to counteract the amount your feet have sunk in the sand. This is one reason you want to take more club if you can. And a great tip I learned from
Claude Harmon is to make sure your arms are fully extended at address. If
your arms are a little slack, they straighten out in the swing and it's easy to
dig into the sand.

3.   **4.**

And sweep the ball off the sand (3 and 4) with a quiet swing.

(*Tony Roberts*)

The most accepted strategy for most amateurs is to play the ball in the center of their stance or even in back of center for this shot. However, I've found more advanced players do better if they put the ball more forward. It eventually makes them better fairway bunker players. If you position the ball back, you'll tend to hit it with a descending blow, and the ball will come out too low. With the ball forward, you have a better chancing of picking or sweeping the ball off the sand, which is what you want to do.

I like our students to imagine they're hitting the ball off a cart path.

You don't want sparks to fly and damage your club. There should be no divot with this shot. I also like them to visualize that they are hitting a three-wood, just sweeping or picking the ball off the sand. Both of these images work very well.

The swing should be quiet, something less than a full swing. There should be a minimum of weight transfer. This is more of an arm swing than anything else—the other reason you want more club in your hands. Another good trick is to visualize a stripe around the equator of the ball, like a range ball, and try to make contact just under that equator line, especially if you consistently hit behind the ball. Maintain good eye contact throughout the swing and just nip the ball out of there.

 HARDPAN

The clubface will tend to open quite dramatically when you are playing this type of full shot. Therefore, be sure to toe the face in a little bit at address, or simply aim left and allow for the fade or push.

If you're playing a pitch shot off hardpan, do just the opposite. Use a square or slightly open clubface and play it almost like a sand shot (which I deal with in the next section). You can try to pick the ball off, as in a normal pitch, but if you are going to err, do it slightly behind the ball. The flange of the club will tend to skid across the hardpan and under the ball, and you'll get an acceptable shot.

The Jim McLean Divide by Two Rule

One of my favorite management tips is the divide by two rule. It comes into play most often after a poor tee shot. The average golfer usually tries for a spectacular recovery and ends up in more trouble or swings much too hard, causing a terrible mis-hit. If, for example, you hit a poor drive on a par-4 hole, don't automatically reach for a three-wood. Let's say you are playing a 380-yard hole and you sky your drive into the right rough only 120 yards off the tee. With 260 yards left, it is highly unlikely you will reach the green. Don't reach for the three-wood. Instead, divide the 260 yards by two. It now becomes apparent that two 130 yard shots will get you home. This is a revelation to most of our school students. They realize that two eight-irons can get the job done. A simple eight-iron shot down the fairway can set them up for a 130-yard shot to the green.

Get in Golf Shape

Certainly a big part of your management game is getting physically fit to reach your golf goals. This, of course, varies widely from golfer to golfer. Yet, by observing good diet rules, exercising, and stretching, you can greatly enhance your ability to do more great things in golf. Almost every tour player is now working out and training on a regular basis. That is a huge change in just the last ten years. You will definitely benefit by becoming stronger and more flexible, not to mention improving your overall health.

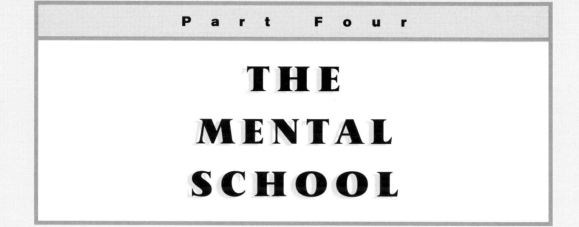

Part Four

THE MENTAL SCHOOL

Many PGA tournament players would claim the game of golf is 90 percent mental. Well, I don't agree with that statement, simply because even the greatest thinkers in the game, such as Jack Nicklaus, still have to set up correctly to the ball and make a good swing to shoot low scores. Actually, I have a quote from Jack that says, "Golf is 50 percent mental, 40 percent setup, and 10 percent swing." This is a nice idea. And you certainly make a good case for that quote. But that mindset will not help you all that much if your swing mechanics and short-game technique are both poor. This is precisely why it is essential that golfers learn the fundamentals of the game first. Without a doubt, however, the mind game—including your attitude, emotional control, relaxation abilities, and visual skills—plays a vital role in your golfing success.

I've given the subject of the mental side a lot of thought, and to be honest, its importance varies from golfer to golfer. I suppose that's because it is difficult to make a judgment as to how much a positive mental attitude will help a player unless the teacher can play a round of golf with that person and see the player react to all sorts of situations. I know only too well that in the case of high handicappers particularly, positive thinking tempts them to try shots they are not capable of hitting. These same players would sometimes be better off thinking defensively, since this mental attitude would discourage them from playing overly dangerous shots during a round and making double and triple bogey on a number of holes.

We tell students at all of our schools that the mental game goes far beyond sheer attitude. Just from the information I have given you so far, you can see how the mental side of the game is directly related to good shot-making and low scoring. It covers a wide scope, involving such areas as shot visualization, swing visualization, relaxation technique, good shot recall, and self-talk.

Now I would like to present some more specific tips, many of which I learned from Dr. Fran Pirozzolo, a neurological psychologist who has been on our staff at the Jim McLean Golf Schools. Dr. Pirozzolo is a member of the National Academy of Sciences committee on techniques to enhance human performance. He has written numerous books on the brain and behavior and on the mental side of golf and its application to the game. He also works on performance enhancement with many PGA Tour pros, with the world champion New York Yankees baseball club, and with world boxing heavyweight champion Evander Holyfield. His experiences in working with elite athletes, along with his nine-year affiliation with the Baylor Medical School in Houston, Texas, have given Fran wonderful insights into constructive thinking.

From Fran Pirozollo, Bob Rotella, Dick Coop, David Cook, and other sports psychologists I've worked with in school situations, I've learned some terrific mental teaching concepts. Here are some of the best.

Go to the Movies

Seeing a shot come to life in your mind's eye before you swing is something that more advanced players must do, and so should you. It narrows your focus and allows you to home in mentally on exactly what you are trying to do with the club you have taken out of your bag. The purer your concentration, the more vivid the image of the ball's flight. Also, when you are mentally focused on a ball flying to a particular area of the fairway or green, you block out any hazards that could cause you to steer the swing and mishit the shot. As talented as Jack Nicklaus is, and regardless of how deeply his game is rooted in the fundamentals, he still believes in preshot visualization, or "going to the movies," as he calls it. In fact, he once commented that he has never hit a shot before first seeing it play perfectly in his head. Nicklaus feels strongly that going through a preshot mental rehearsal prompts the mind to send a message to the body, so that by the time he addresses the ball, his shoulders, arms, hands, wrists, legs, and feet are well prepared to meet their job description and do what it takes to make the proper swing.

Nicklaus is known as one of the game's greatest fundamentalists. He usually plays his bread-and-butter fade. Other players, such as Tiger Woods and Phil Mickelson, are known as more imaginative shot-makers. These young superstars are renowned for their creative shots—so much so that you never know what shot they are going to play. Consequently, they may have to be even more visual than Nicklaus in their mental preparation.

Rehearse Your Swing

As well as Nicklaus, Woods, Mickelson, and other pros play, they like to see themselves making the ideal swing in their mind before they swing. This mental rehearsal helps raise their level of confidence, which is especially helpful on a day when things are not going as planned on the golf course.

Some players, such as Davis Love, benefit from concentrating very intently on making a practice swing that matches the swing they are trying to put on the ball. This is something we encourage our students to do, particularly since most of them make a haphazard practice swing, or one that does not relate to the shot at hand. Often amateurs make an overly lazy, extra-short action. As I explain to them, this is why they sometimes feel lost or fearful standing over the ball. Their behavior is analogous to that of an actor who hasn't rehearsed his lines. There is no value in this type of negative preparation, so make it part of your routine to see yourself mentally making the best swing you are capable of making. Then make a practice motion that encourages all the good things you hope to achieve.

How to Overcome the First-Tee Jitters

To play a good game of golf, you must focus at the proper times from the first hole to the final putt of the round. However, what you do on the first hole will often have just a little more importance to how you perform on the remaining seventeen holes. A good start sets a positive tone for the day. So think of the first hole as a round all by itself. In the two years I worked extensively with Hal Sutton, I learned some fantastic mental keys. One of the best was the advice Hal got directly from Jack Nicklaus, regarding the opening tee shot. Jack thought this was the most important shot of the day and gave extra attention in his preparation. A technique Hal used was getting to the first tee ten minutes prior to his start time. Hal uses this extra few minutes to relax, slow down, and get extra ready for the opening shot.

Many amateurs I speak to are amazed after coming back from a pro event. They are surprised that the majority of professionals hit such solid and accurate drives off the first tee. I guess they feel this way because to them the first tee shot is extremely frightening. Some students tell me that they have such first-tee jitters they are actually happy when they simply make contact with the ball. I understand this fear, because I've been there, teeing it up at the Masters or in a U.S. Open. I realize that the first tee shot plays on your nerves. In fact, I still experience butterflies in my stomach when I tee up on the first hole of a tournament. That's because the first tee area is usually especially active and crowded. Many times it is very close to the range or the clubhouse. With other golfers in the vicinity, negative thoughts are bound to enter your mind.

It's okay to be a little bit nervous, since that signals adrenaline flow and an enhanced level of awareness, but you can't let that nervousness overcome you.

We have learned some excellent techniques to let you take control of the situation and prevent tension and nervousness from causing a very bad shot. One technique involves visually recalling a good drive you hit off the first tee in the past. You can recall a good opening drive on any course. Adopt this mental strategy. Really concentrate, so that you can clearly picture a well-hit accurate drive, and do it over and over. You will alleviate anxiety, and the muscles in your body will begin to relax, readying you to make a nice, accelerating golf swing.

Another technique is to go patiently through your routine. Make a nice fluid practice swing, pick out a landing spot, and, as Jackie Burke taught me, make believe you are hitting into the Atlantic Ocean. In other words, let go and don't attempt to steer the ball. Burke's thought has helped me hit solid drives off the first tee in many tournaments or big matches, mainly because it encourages me to make a free swing. That's why I pass it on to my students. All of our Master Instructors use this concept, or similar ideas, to help students relax, particularly on their opening shot, when anxiety is at a high pitch.

How to Shake Off a Mistake

Everyone makes a silly mistake at times during a round. You, I am sure, have wanted to kick yourself for either hitting the wrong club, trying to carry a water hazard that required your A-game shot, or three-putted from only 10 feet because you tried to knock a bold downhill slider in the cup. At these times during the game, it is easy to lose your cool. The tendency is to give up completely, stand up on the next tee, and try to knock the cover off the ball, or play overly aggressively and attack the flag in an attempt to score birdies and make up ground. Whatever, you tend to do something that makes the situation worse and undermines your ability to shoot the best score you can.

I am very aware that all golfers make these mistakes from time to time, because I have made the very same mistakes. Of course, I have also watched all kinds of players fall victim to mental errors, either while being paired with them in a tournament or while giving them a playing lesson. Stupid mistakes are a fact of life on the golf course. The secret is to lessen the errors you make by thinking strategically and recovering quickly when you do make them. The best way I know of to turn my game around after making an on-course mistake is to talk to myself. "Okay, you gambled and you lost. Now let's think clearly and smartly and avoid compounding the mistakes" is my kind of self-talk. It's what you might call immediate damage control. To help me get back on track, I try to recall another occasion when I made a similar mistake, or got off to the same bad start on the opening holes, then ended up shooting a great round.

Golf, as we all know, parallels life. One day you wake up feeling great and things go badly for you, while another day you wake up feeling lousy and everything works in your favor. The great mind players are those who never let themselves get too excited when things go in their favor or depressed when things work against them. Many top players do better when they have no expectations and they rarely predict how they will do in a particular championship round. A big part of the success Fred Couples enjoys can be credited to his relaxed mental attitude; he's so low-key and expressionless that when he walks off a green, you can't tell whether he just made double eagle or double bogey. David Duval and Anika Sorenstam do the same thing. The real advantage of this laidback mindset is that it prevents you from getting too upset about a mistake—so upset that you go on a suicide mission for the rest of the round, doing such destructive things as trying to drive the ball over the corner of doglegs, attempting to hit a wood over a high-lipped bunker, or trying to ram 60-foot putts in the center of the cup.

Don't Add Your Score Until It's Over

When it comes to scoring and the mental game, certainly one of the biggest errors amateurs make is counting their score. Beginners typically make this mistake, and they put more pressure on themselves the second they finish figuring out how they are doing and discover they are well ahead of their best-ever score. This is one of the fastest ways to take yourself out of your comfort zone. I do not mean to single out novices. Mid-handicap players who have a chance to break 80 also freak out. As for low-handicap players, I've seen them panic when they are finally in position to break par. In fact, I'm sure we have all seen good players relax as soon as they make a high score on a hole that ruins their under-par game. They relax because they could not handle the situation and now no longer have to deal with the pressure of trying to hang on and go low. This is a natural reaction we all must overcome as we move our game to a higher, more sophisticated level.

Whatever handicap you play to, try not to think ahead to difficult holes coming up, or to the score you have the chance of shooting at the completion of the round. Play one hole at a time, one shot at a time, concentrating at an even level from tee to green. That's something I have learned from working with many sports psychologists. Also, try something I often teach to my students. Whichever tees you normally play, tee up from the forward tees the next time you play a game. Playing a shorter course and making more pars and birdies will help you mentally get accustomed to going low, or handling yourself in low-score conditions. I know it is ironic: our goal is to shoot low scores, but when things go well we often lose control and become anxious. I am afraid this is the nature of the beast. So work on constructive ways to conquer your fears and rise to the occasion.

Good Planning Can Make You More Confident

I always enjoy going to a range and watching amateur golfers practice. I learn a lot about players' weaknesses there, then go back home and try to find ways to help golfers break their bad habits. Naturally, my major concern is for my students, who come to me for private lessons or visit my schools. Some of the most important things we cover in our training session with our assistant instructors follow.

The majority of players who visit the range before a round always seem to be in a rush and have no plan whatsoever. I know that life can be hectic, and also that it is often difficult to leave enough preparatory time available. Still, if you take the time to arrange a friendly game of golf, or if you are scheduled to play in a match, be smart and take care of your home duties and business affairs ahead of time. If possible, and I know that sometimes it is not, you can arrive at the course about an hour before your tee time. All accomplished players arrive at the course with plenty of time to spare. Many are so organized that they give themselves the luxury of driving extra slowly to the course, so they can quietly gather their thoughts in private. A player might even go into the locker room and purposely tie her shoes slowly to promote relaxation. Next, with the help of her caddie, a Tour player will make sure she has sleeves of new balls, tees, towels, extra gloves, an umbrella in case it rains, and a Band-Aid in case she gets a blister on her hands from practicing so hard. All this careful planning makes you more poised and confident.

The main purpose of planning ahead concerns practice. Ideally, you want to give yourself enough time to be able to practice efficiently. That means hitting balls with a purpose. You may try going through the bag, hitting all the shots that you feel you will have to play on the course. For example, you might decide that many holes are better suited to a draw. Consequently, you should imagine playing a particular dogleg left. Then, on the range, pull out your driver, go through your preswing routine, visualize a right-to-left power-draw shot, make the setup adjustments necessary for playing that shot, then go ahead and hit it. Go through several key holes and rehearse all the shots you will have to play from tee to green, including special shots with an iron, such as a knockdown or running pitch. This is how you can prepare like the best players in the game.

Our instructors teach students to learn from the greatest players. We encourage them always to practice with a purpose, because the better prepared you are in practice, the more likely you are to stand up on the first tee and hit a good shot and to continue playing confidently for the entire round.

When you get to the course early, you can also give yourself the luxury of going to the sand bunker, the chipping green, and the putting green. That usually means you will be one up on your opponent before the game begins and shoot a good score. Again, be well organized in your life, so that you can give yourself the best chance of accomplishing your on-course goals.

For many years at our schools, we have taught an opposite pre-round practice approach. That is, go to the putting green first, then to the range, and then directly to the first tee. This accomplishes many things. First it makes certain you practice putting. Second, it allows you to go directly to the first tee warmed up and ready to go.

Whenever Possible, Practice the Tough Shots

The next time you get a chance, go to your home course in the quiet of an afternoon and practice the shots that scare you. Practice hitting balls out of fairway bunkers, hitting woods and irons out of deep rough, hitting balls from under and over trees, hitting shots out of buried lies in the bunker; even try short shots out of water with half of the ball submerged. By practicing these shots, you will be better able to hit them on the course. Moreover, you will gain so much confidence that when you stand on the tee or over an approach shot, you will be less likely to steer the swing, Instead, you will make a free swing, because you know if you land in trouble, you will be able to get out of it.

This certainly is one of the great advantages we have at our golf schools. While playing with a professional, each student is taught how to hit various difficult recovery shots. These little tips help students shoot lower scores when they return home. Often it's not the new swing but the new thinking that helps.

Personalize Your Swing Cues

In the initial stages of learning to swing correctly, you will be bombarded with a lot of information. So many tips will be given to you that if you are not careful, you will suffer from paralysis by analysis. In other words, you must avoid going through a long checklist of swing thoughts every time you stand up to the ball to hit a shot, or else you will freeze over the ball, then make a tense, robotic swing that lacks rhythm. We say "too much information is often worse than no information."

For example, many golfers find that if they start the club back correctly, the rest of the pieces fall into place automatically, much as one domino's falling over knocks the rest of them down. Try to develop a singular mental cue to trigger the backswing, then let the rest of the swing happen. If you feel that your backswing is good but you have trouble swinging through the ball, devise your own personal downswing cue, such as "make a lateral hip shift." One backswing thought and one downswing thought are usually enough for any golfer.

It's important to know that swing cues are used often by the pros. In fact, depending on how they are playing, they may use one or more mental swing cues during a round. The important thing is to think of this cue before you swing, or even whisper it to yourself. Be imaginative in the use of these cues.

To help you let loose mentally, here are some cues used by various pros, which I have incorporated into my teaching. To promote a strong turning action, Greg Norman thinks "RPB," which is his signal to turn his right pocket back. To keep the clubface square to the target, Ken Venturi thinks "Back of my left hand is a second clubface." At impact, his goal is to have the clubface and the back of the hand line up. Curtis Strange thinks "Shortstop position" to help him set up in a relaxed, flexed, ready position at address. To make sure that she completes her backswing, Nancy Lopez thinks "Wait at the top." The list goes on. The point is, use one or two swing cues that will allow the rest of the swing to operate virtually all on its own.

I believe strongly in swing thoughts versus having no thoughts at all as you stand over the ball. A positive swing key tends to relax the golfer and tune him or her into executing a solid swing action. No swing thoughts tend to allow for a wandering mindset.

How to Trigger a Focused Mental Attitude

If you treat golf mostly as a social outing, then it is perfectly okay to make the round fun for yourself and others. But if you are really interested in trying to improve as a player and lower your handicap, you must find ways to put yourself in a mental cocoon for the twenty or thirty seconds it takes to prepare and focus totally on each shot during your round. In between shots, it's fine to relax and talk with your playing partners. That's what makes golf such a great game.

You must try to find some way to trigger serious mental focus when it comes time to hit your shot—something to stop your mind from wandering. Pull on your pant leg, snap a rubber band looped around your wrist, readjust your glasses, pull on the brim of your hat, or open and close the Velcro on your glove. Do whatever you choose, as long as it brings your mind into focus. Often a physical cue gets your mind back into the game, signaling that it's time to execute your preshot routine and make your best swing.

Play According to Your Personality

If you are a Type A person who likes to do most things quickly, then let that trait hold true on the course. In our golf schools, we meet people who play badly because they try to be somebody else on the course. Do you think that Tom Watson would play as well as he does if he suddenly took more time over every shot? The answer is no. By the same token, Jack Nicklaus could never play as well as he does if he played shots as quickly as Watson. The key to success is to know who you are and hold to that personality on the course.

Don't Be Afraid of Change

There are basically two kinds of players: analytical, mechanical players and intuitive players. Whichever category you fall into, don't be afraid to change in the middle of the round if your game goes sour.

If thinking out your technique is not working, address the ball with a clean mental slate. Just get up and hit the ball, off the tee and on approach shots.

If you are an intuitive player and your game goes south, try concentrating on the fundamentals of grip, stance, aim, and alignment. Pay close attention to yardage markers and the course situation at hand. Also, spend more time contemplating club selection and choice of shot.

You'll discover that just by changing your habits, you will be more free-spirited in your approach, and more relaxed. That's because you don't have any high expectations about shooting a great score.

Relaxation Helps Create a Positive Mental Attitude

Many teachers say that it is important to develop a positive mental attitude, because this state of mind makes you more relaxed. I believe that if you can get yourself to relax, you will become more positive. To promote relaxation, try whistling a tune like Fuzzy Zoeller does, taking time in between shots to look at the scenery and thank God you are able to play this great game. Hum a favorite tune, or think of your wife and kids and the fun you have together. We tell our students these things while giving them playing lessons, and we watch their game improve. This happens because putting yourself in a relaxed mode often improves your confidence, and allows you to get into the flow.

Use Your Imagination

Whenever you face a pitch over water, imagine instead that you are hitting shots at targets on the driving range. Pretend that there is nothing but grass between your ball and the hole. Before you swing, actually imagine the practice setting, particularly one green on the range with a bright yellow or red flag. This mental trickery may be all you need to go from a negative mental attitude to a positive one.

How to Avoid Stress in the Sand

Many amateurs panic when facing a shot in sand. I know this is because they have poor technique and have experienced many disappointing outcomes. Yet even if you have the proper technique, you must above all remain relaxed.

This is a relatively simple shot to play if you just remember to open the face of a sand wedge and use the technique I've described, depending on the distance of the shot and the lip you have to carry. The higher the lip and the shorter the shot, the farther you stand from the ball and the more open the clubface. Remember, you need the proper technique to feel confident. Review the short-game school, where I discuss the ins and outs of good sand play, and take the time to practice this crucial recovery shot. As I've said, having a strong bunker game will help your iron play, because you'll lose the fear of missing greens.

Visualize a Line

All top putters I've interviewed visualize some type of line to their target. Some see a wide white road, others see a dark narrow dew line. Still others see a dotted line or a set of rails. There is probably no limit to the visual images that can work. My point here is to encourage you to work on imagery. Try different ideas and experiment with mind pictures. A clear image builds tremendous confidence.

Chip to a Bucket

I think you'll agree that failing to get the ball up and in from just off the green after hitting an approach directly over the pin onto the back fringe is one of the most frustrating experiences in golf. If you have a problem hitting chips close to the cup, imagine the hole as a big bucket. This will get you thinking about holing the chip instead of trying to steer the shot close to the cup. A larger target also tends to relax almost everyone.

Know That Golf Is Not a Game That Can Be Perfected

If you've played this game for some time, you know that no matter how well you play on a particular day, you could have always played better. This is because golf is a highly complex game that brings in the element of luck and the bad and good bounce. No matter how well you swing, you often have to deal with wind and rain. You will also have to face a bad lie, owing to a bad shot or a bad break. So heed these words of Jackie Burke: "Be prepared to scramble, right from the first tee." This is great advice, because it readies you to face adversity and use your mental toughness to look at every difficult on-course situation as a challenge.

Keep "If" and "Should" Out of Your Vocabulary

I'll bet there have been times out on the course when you have heard your playing partners make statements like these: "If that green wasn't so hard, the ball would have finished stiff to the flag." "I should have laid up." "If that green wasn't so slow, I would have holed that putt." Mature golfers don't let "if" and "should" into their vocabulary when they are playing a round. They realize that there are no second chances on the course, so it is not worth it to cry over spilt milk. Adopt the same attitude. If you make a mistake that costs you a shot or shots, accept the consequences and move on to the next hole. Get back in the present moment and let go of the past disappointment.

Adopting the Right Attitude

If you are a golfer who does not believe in yourself, I want you to try to remember these performance-enhancing attitudes, which are taught at our schools by Dr. Pirozzolo:

- Trust yourself.
- Thrive on the challenge of trying to conquer the course.
- Have fun.
- Play in the present tense.
- Be relaxed.
- Stay focused on the shot situation.
- Be performance-oriented.

Fight Off the Negatives

Our teachers meet students all the time who are their own worst enemies. And I'm not just talking about high handicappers. Often a good player will have a good round going, then manage to lose control because of negative thoughts. Don't ever accept these thoughts. Fight them off. For example, the next time you face a tough shot, simply whisper this to yourself: "I've got this shot in my bag, and I know it, so nothing is going to stop me from pulling it off." We all know this positive self-talk helps. Try not to forget it when the going gets tough.

Stay Mentally in the Hole

While giving a playing lesson at our schools, we might see a student give up after hitting a topped drive on a par 5 hole. Don't ever give up. Simply put all of your mental energy and power of concentration into making the next shot count, then the next, then the next, then the next. And you know what? Even after a topped tee shot, you will often still have a chance to record a par on your card.

Match Play Magic

When many golfers play a head-to-head match, they have a habit of playing the opponent instead of the golf course. I make sure I let my students know that this attitude can cause them to lose. Don't focus too much on your opponent, no matter what shot he or she hits, or you'll put unnecessary pressure on yourself. And whatever you do, don't let up mentally after your opponent hits a bad shot, or else you'll probably hit one yourself. Please pretend that you are playing the course and trying to turn in a good medal score. Concentrate on your shots and only your shots. Trust me, this attitude will take you to the winner's circle.

Part Five

THE POWER SCHOOL

Nowadays, there is a bigger attraction to power than ever before in the history of the game. This is true because of the huge forward strides that have been taken in the world of equipment technology. The golf ball is traveling farther than ever before because of more sophisticated construction, but it is also the golf club that has really brought the game into a new dimension. The standard length, persimmon headed drivers that were once in practically every golfer's bag have for some time been virtually anachronistic. The new extra-long, graphite-shafted, titanium-headed drivers featuring gigantic heads are hot—so hot that the way things are going, there will be no looking back.

What I find so ironic in the face of this technological boom is that many average club golfers are not hitting the ball all that much farther, or straighter, in spite of the wider sweet-spot element of the clubface and the advances in club design. It's a fact that golfers are buying everything on the market, too. In fact, when teaching at one of my power schools, I see everything in golfers' bags, from Spalding's Intimidator, to Callaway's Big Bertha, to Titleist's 975, to Taylor Made's Bubble, to Orlimar's Tri-Metal driver. Students prove to me all the time that they are not afraid to spend money on the most expensive clubs on the market. Sadly, though, they also prove to me that they should concentrate more on learning the fundamentals of a power swing by investing in a few lessons.

If one of your goals is to hit the ball powerfully and on-target, you must face up to one fact: you can't buy power simply by purchasing a big-bucks driver. You need the combination of a good club and a good swing in order to evolve into a consistent power-control hitter. Every pro and single-figure golfer knows this is true, and that is why those players spend a few hours each week practicing what they learned from their teacher.

In our power schools, we teach individuals to set up in a particular way so they build a firm foundation for promoting a strong, balanced swinging action. After that, we get into the ins and outs of the backswing and downswing, with the major focus on how to load and unload power. What is so special about our schools is that all of us who teach have carefully studied and analyzed the great power swings of past and present Tour professionals and great amateurs throughout history. We've looked at still photographs, swing sequences, and videotape of long-hitting pros, including George Bayer, Sam Snead, Ben Hogan, Fred Couples, Davis Love, David Duval, John Daly, and, of course, Tiger Woods. Additionally, we've analyzed the swings of powerful amateurs, such as Grand Slam winner Bobby Jones, Matt Kuchar, the 1997 U.S. Amateur champion, and Sergio Garcia, the 1998 British Amateur champion, who many golf experts say hits the ball nearly as far as Tiger. We've picked all these swings apart and determined the common power traits among them. Ultimately, our goal is to get our students to incorporate some or all of these power-generating elements into their existing swing technique, so they increase their clubhead speed while increasing the number of times they put the clubface squarely on the ball.

The step-by-step process we use has been proven to work. I can proudly say that more than 95 percent of the students who visit our schools leave hitting the ball at least 10 yards longer than they did before they came. I would like to say that this improvement is due solely to my fellow instructors and me. Yet that is by no means true. A lot of the success of our power schools has to do with the individuals themselves. Most of them arrive totally frustrated, because they have tried seemingly every tip in the book and every driver on the market, with little success. Because of this frustration, the second they show up on the tee they want to hit balls, thinking that they might quickly learn one secret that will solve all their driving problems. I explain that the road to power driving is gradual, and I tell them that I do not allow them to hit balls until they can prove that they can set up correctly over and over. Then, and only then, do they start accepting that good hard honest work is the only path to improvement. Along the way, our professionals offer them drills and tell them anecdotes about the pros we have taught, which makes the learning process more fun. But we are always honest, explaining that some students may get worse before they get better, owing to the drastic changes they will make in their present technique. We also tell them that if they are willing to work hard, they will develop long-lasting power-driving habits. To their credit, it is at this point that they buckle down and never look back at their past driving problems.

You too will have to be prepared to let go of old habits and work extra hard to improve. Throughout your entire time at my at-home power school, you will be asked to change the way you address the ball and swing. Heed my instructions, no matter how uncomfortable they make you feel. Although my new keys may take you out of your comfort zone and may initially make it difficult to make center contact, I guarantee that once they become second nature, you will see a huge transformation in your driving game. You will hit the ball much longer and straighter, with the real bonus of a feeling of ease and effortlessness in your swing. The chief reason for this new rhythmic flow in your swing will be the improved coordination between the movement of your body and the movement of the golf club. I promise that you will feel like you are swinging more easily, while in fact the club will move faster and faster as it approaches the ball, with its face consistently spanking the back-center portion of the ball.

As you learn each new power key, such as taking a wider stance or turning your shoulders far more than your hips, try to feel the action. Too often, students listen to my instructions but learn them only in their head. To be a good student, you must do more than comprehend the elements of good form. You must experience each and every physical sensation involved and practice them, so that you are better able to repeat the action over and over on a regular basis—and so you can return to good form quickly after falling into a slump.

Some teachers and scientists say there is no such thing as muscle

227

memory, and that might very well be technically true. All the same, I cannot impress upon you enough the importance of learning the correct feel of a good setup and swing by doing drills on the practice tee or in your home. If you internalize these vital positions through diligent and honest practice sessions, your body will respond virtually automatically when you swing. Because this shadowing technique works, you will not freeze over the ball and employ an overly mechanical or robotic swing. Consequently, you will perform better under pressure, when playing a casual Nassau match or teeing up in your club championship.

The secrets to my power address, power backswing, and power downswing follow. Learn them first, then make them automatic with hard practice.

The Power Address

All you have to do is go down to your local golf course on a weekend to confirm that the setup truly does determine the motion. Basically, you'll see that those players who slice or duck-hook the ball set up very differently from pros who hit the ball a long way. Almost all pros look identical at address, and all power hitters share a number of fundamentals, involving stance width, feet position, ball placement, head position, weight distribution, and hand position. They also tend to tee the ball up in pretty much the same way.

Power hitters tee the ball up high, so that a little more than half the ball is above the top of the clubface. They also move their left foot more forward than normal, well outside the left shoulder. This is a very important detail for you to check. A small adjustment to your stance at address helps you establish a wide base that in turn helps promote an elongated takeaway and wide backswing arc. Further, this unique setup position helps restrain hip action in the backswing. Further still, it makes the weight shift to your left leg and side on the downswing far easier to do.

Ken Venturi taught me that there are other advantages to standing with your feet spread several inches wider than the width of your shoulders. Venturi played often with the ultimate ball-striker, Ben Hogan, who was very cautious about sharing his intimate swing secrets. He did, however, pass many tips on to Venturi, who over the years passed them on to me. I in turn pass many of them on to those who come to my power schools or take these lessons in book form.

According to Venturi, the wide base helps promote a low center of gravity for added body stability, a shallower swing, and an extended flat spot through the impact zone. This elongated flat spot is especially important, because it allows you to keep the club on the ball a split second longer as you hit through the ball, ensuring powerfully accurate hits. Playing from an extra-wide stance is also better because it enhances your balance. And when you shift forward from a broad base and swing through impact, you are able to put all your weight behind the shot, much as a boxer moves forward to punch his opponent with a right cross.

To take full advantage of the flat spot in your shallow driver swing, play the ball off the left heel, as Venturi and other top instructors advise. When you position the ball forward in the stance, you set yourself up to connect with it as the club is moving slightly upward through impact. As a result, the ball is propelled into the air quickly, as it takes off, before it flattens out into a line drive. This trajectory pays great dividends with respect to distance, for the simple reason that once the ball touches down on the fairway, it will be hot and usually run quite a long way.

Many power-fade players set their feet, and sometimes their body, open to the target line or aiming slightly left. However, I think you will give yourself the best possible chance of making a good swing and returning the club squarely to the ball at impact if you take a square setup.

Students at our power schools are also taught to place their right foot pretty much perpendicular to the target line, which prevents the hips from turning too far and decreasing their personal X factor, which I'll explain later in this section. We also instruct students to turn their left foot outward between 20 and 30 degrees, since this position increases the speed of the hip rotation through the ball. That's a major plus, because all things being equal, the faster the hips clear in the hitting area, the faster the club moves, the more solidly the club meets the ball, and the farther the ball flies.

The power posture is very similar to that for any other swing. Just make sure to tilt your spine about 10 degrees away from the target, set your left hip slightly above your right hip, angle your head back slightly and position it behind the ball, and drop your right shoulder just a little. This helps you hit the ball powerfully on the upswing.

Another important feature of the address concerns the position of the hands. Although there have been great players who set up with their hands behind the ball (notably Hogan) and those who set them slightly ahead (notably Nicklaus), I recommend that you line your hands up with the ball. It's important for the clubshaft to be nearly straight up and down, at a 90-degree angle. My experience at our power schools indicates that this in-line position enables golfers to swing the club on the correct path and plane more consistently. Most players who set their hands behind the ball tend to take the club away to the outside. Players who set their hands well ahead of the ball tend to take the club away more to the inside. While I am on the subject of the hands, be sure to grip the club at about three or four on our one-to-ten scale of pressure. Light arms and hands translates into speed for you.

The position of your arms at address is also a critical link to employing a technically sound power swing. When standing to the ball, draw an imaginary line through the center of your forearms running parallel to the target line. Don't ever let your right forearm drop under or lift over your left forearm, or you will probably swing the club along an improper path and mishit the ball. Don't make the mistake of letting your right elbow rest against your right side, either, for that is a very weak position. Letting the right elbow hug your side on the backswing causes a huge power leak in your swing. Get in the habit of setting up with your right elbow free and away from your body, since this position encourages a free arm-club backswing action, a wide arc, and a resulting strong turn of the body. Relaxation of the arms is crucial too. Therefore, try imagining that your arms are two ropes hanging from your body, both in an extended but not taut position. This promotes relaxed muscles and arm speed.

Since the correct address position is so vital to producing a power swing and solid drives, I advise you to rehearse your setup in front of a mirror. Look at it from different angles to make sure you are addressing the ball as you think you are. Alternatively, have a friend check your setup or videotape your address. The reason I am being so forceful about this off-course practice is because even the greatest players in the world can fall into a driving slump because of one small fault in the setup.

The Power Backswing Action

The backswing action for more distance—indeed, the entire swing—is essentially the same as I described in the section on the eight-step swing in the full-swing school. However, the essence of generating power during the first half of the swing involves the accentuation of an ingredient called the X factor. Let's examine that more fully.

Let me begin with a little history of just how this vital swing key was discovered. While traveling around the world to analyze the game's most talented professionals and teachers, in search of the secrets to golf instruction, I saw one common denominator in the modern power hitters. The most powerful hitters seemed to restrict their backswing hip turn while coiling the upper body tremendously. Generations of golfers have been taught the opposite: to coil the hips and shoulders as far as possible to get maximum power. Still, I came up with a very interesting concept of the four turns of the body as I studied swinging on video. I then used this new concept in writing several major pieces for *Golf* magazine.

I decided to seek the help of Mike McTeigue, a golf professional who said that he could test golfers using a SportSense Swing Motion Trainer, which literally strapped a player in while he swung. The unit on the player's back would send information to a computer, which would produce data on the degree of shoulder and hip turn in the swing. Consequently, I arranged to test the Tour players at the Doral Ryder Open.

Mike collected the data and sent me the original report. Every long hitter we tested had a big differential between the amount of shoulder and hip turn at the top of the swing. We called that differential "the gap." In contrast, the short hitters had much smaller gaps. It was a fascinating comparison. The data revealed that John Daly, at the time the PGA Tour's longest hitter, had the highest differential. He turned his shoulders 114 degrees and his hips 66, for a differential or gap of 48, the highest on Tour. One of the shortest hitters, Mike Reid, had a gap of only 26, turning his shoulders 88 degrees and his hips 62 degrees. We confirmed that a big turn was not the chief key to generating power. The key to creating power rests in the gap numbers—the X Factor.

To improve their gap, most golfers need to resist lower body action in the move away from the ball. If you have the flexibility to make a strong shoulder turn, be sure to keep your hip turn restricted. Again, one way to encourage a restricted hip turn is to set up with your right foot square to the target line. Another way is to make sure you keep your right knee flexed during the backswing.

In reading this description of the value of hip turn restriction, I do not want you to get the wrong impression. I'm not saying that the hips don't turn—far from it. I recommend that the hips turn between 40 and 65 degrees. If you feel that your hip turn is too restricted, try turning your right foot outward slightly, away from the target line. The model on full swings is a 100-degree shoulder turn and a 60-degree hip turn. That's a huge 40-degree difference.

If you are not very flexible and need to increase your shoulder turn in order to increase your differential, allow your left heel to be pulled off the ground on the backswing. Do not consciously lift it up. Just let it rise off the ground as you turn your body and shift your weight onto your right foot and leg.

At the top of the swing, make sure that your left shoulder is behind the ball. If that is not the case, you have not coiled correctly. Your weight should be over your right foot, more toward the inside heel. If it goes to the outside of the foot or toward the toes, your balance will suffer. Your chin should have rotated as far as it can away from the target. Some power hitters turn the chin as much as 45 degrees; the average is 20 to 25 degrees. It's important that your left arm be extended but not stiff or tense. Remember, I mentioned four body turns. Those turns are (1) the angle between your knees at the top of the backswing; (2) hip turn; (3) shoulder turn; and (4) the amount of head turn. All four turns contribute to your ability either to increase or to decrease your turning action. This is how you max out your coil potential.

The Power Downswing Action

If you have followed our power school lessons thus far, you should experience the same thing that happens to students at our schools: they get the feeling that they are being pulled through the ball by outside forces. The reason is that by the time the end of the school rolls around, they know exactly how to create power on the backswing. Further, they know how to make the laws of physics work for them. In short, they are so wound up at the top they cannot help being pulled through the impact zone. Still, they are helped to swing their hands, arms, and club through impact by an important key—a lateral shift action of the hips that shifts weight to the left side, your main pivot point for making the downswing.

The mechanics of the downswing are essentially the same as those I discussed in the full-swing school, but let's look at them again in relation to the X Factor. First, I do not want to give the impression that you make a full stop at the top, then start down. The entire swing should be one flowing, uninterrupted motion. Nonetheless, a fraction of a pause does occur at the top. This may also be termed a change in direction. Whatever way you describe it, the clubhead keeps traveling back while the lower body or hips nudge forward.

To relate the X Factor to the mechanics of the downswing, understand that the average Tour player arrives at the top with a gap between the shoulders and hips of more than 30 degrees. But, interestingly, by impact there is a gap of only about 10 degrees, or less. This means that the upper body has somehow caught up to the hips by impact. If you are wondering how we got these figures, they were determined by strapping professionals into the Sports Motion Trainer once again. The average Tour player's upper body—his shoulders—was 87 degrees closed at the top of the swing. At impact, his upper body was 26 degrees open. Add those up and you discover that the upper body traveled 113 degrees from the top of the swing to impact. The average Tour player's hips were 55 degrees closed at the top of the swing. At impact, his hips were 32 degrees open, since they rotated or cleared to the left of target. That means the hips traveled a total distance of 87 degrees.

I know it is hard to understand that the upper body catches up to the hips, because the hips get a head start when you nudge them toward the target at the start of the downswing. "So how does this happen?" you ask. I wondered the same thing, but after close analysis and a lot of hard thinking, I came up with the answer. As I reported in the August 1993 cover story in *Golf* magazine, the upper body rotates around a fixed axis, the spine. The hips rotate around two axes, the right leg on the backswing and the left leg on the follow-through. This, then, is the reason. The change is the result of the lateral move toward the target. Therefore, don't think of the hips as merely turning; they must shift laterally, as I have pointed out, and then rotate. The lateral shift recenters your weight and triggers the full weight transfer from right to left. In the space of time it takes to shift just slightly, the upper body has a chance to catch up. When all this technical jargon is sorted out, it means that in order to close the gap, as all power hitters do on the downswing, you must not only move your hips laterally, you must allow them to rotate around your left leg, or front pivot point.

The true secret to the X Factor and to power is keeping your upper body tightly wound up while you initiate the movement of your hips laterally toward the target. This single key will maximize your differential so you can thrust the upper body through impact and powerfully slam the gap closed.

Once your hips are activated, the rest of the downswing, including the follow-through and finish, operates essentially on automatic pilot. The hands, arms, and club fall downward while the right shoulder lowers. Weight keeps shifting to the left leg while the hips clear more to the left. The club moves into the delivery position I described earlier and finally to and through the ball, into the follow-through and finish positions.

Power Drills

At our power schools, we try to provide students with knowledge about the setup and swing that will allow them consistently to hit the ball longer. To be honest, since most players who visit us have been exposed to a lot of misinformation, we have to work hard to help them clear their heads of many wrong swing thoughts and be able to internalize new, good body and club positions. By breaking the swing down into small, understandable steps, we almost always make substantial improvements.

This will provide new technical information that you don't necessarily need to know. However, you must understand where your mistakes are made. You need to see the logic behind it; you need to believe it; you need to trust it. Our major concern is to see our students fully through the learning process, so they find specific ways to incorporate the correct moves into their bodies. One of the best ways in which we get students to feel the correct positions that promote power is to have them do drills, which is what I want you to do. As experience has shown, drills expedite the learning process and make it more fun. For this reason, eight of my favorite drills—the very same ones used at our power schools to help golfers learn the best backswing and downswing positions—follow. All have been proven to work wonders, so practice them at your course or in your own back yard.

 ## LEARNING TO QUIET THE WRISTS

The last thing you want to do at the start of the swing is to immediately cock your wrists. A too-early set drains power out of your swing, because it prevents you from extending the club back in the takeaway and creating a wide swing arc.

To train the wrists to stay passive for the first part of the takeaway, set up with the club's butt end in the center of your chest. Next, practice your move away from the ball. The clubhead will move approximately 3 feet. This one simple drill will allow you to feel immediately the correct sensation of quiet wrists. Do it often to capture the feel.

Incorporate this shoulder-controlled takeaway into your swing and you'll build an easy-to-repeat power swing.

 ## TWENTY IN A ROW

One of the quickest ways to lose distance is to let the body sway so far to the right on the backswing that weight shifts to the outside of the right foot. This faulty move causes you to lose your balance and mis-hit the shot.

Another mistake involving body action happens on the downswing. The player's right shoulder juts outward, causing him to pull the club across the ball through impact. This fault usually forces you to hit a pull-slice shot.

The point I am making here is that power can leak out of the swing if you rely too heavily on the body to generate clubhead speed. The twenty-in-a-row drill will support the fact that the arms and hands also produce clubhead speed on the downswing. If you overuse the upper body, practicing this drill will help you learn the correct feeling of letting your body respond to the swinging of your hands and arms, not the other way around.

Take your normal driver address. Make twenty straight swings, never stopping to pause and keeping your feet very low to the ground to help you restrict body action and feel how the arms and hands work in time to create power. It's a fantastic drill to create a true arc and a lot more speed in the swing.

BUILDING LEFT-ARM STRENGTH AND SUPER CONTROL

There is no doubt that the right hand plays a huge role in helping a player generate high clubhead speed and hit the ball powerfully. But many amateurs overuse their right hand at the wrong time. In many cases, the fault is a misunderstanding of the release action. Many players have heard that the right hand and arm must turn over the left. That's not exactly true; this action does not occur until after impact.

To allow the right hand to come into play at the right time and to return the clubface squarely to the ball at impact, the left hand and arm must serve as a guide during the swing. This drill will help you learn the correct motion.

Grip a seven-iron in your left hand and let your right hand and arm hang down normally, or put your right hand behind your back. Take the club back to the halfway point, concentrating on letting the clubface fan open. Next, hit the ball, letting your left elbow fold after the ball has been struck.

You will probably hit your first few shots off to the right. However, stay with this drill, because it will train you to swing the club on the correct path and return its face squarely and powerfully to the ball with your left arm and hand. Once you practice this drill and get the hang of hitting solid shots, incorporate the correct left-sided actions into your driver swing.

STRENGTHENING YOUR TURN

The ancient tip "Turn your left shoulder under your chin" tends to cause a player to dip, or reverse pivot—to leave her weight on the left side at the top of the swing and on the right foot at impact. I also think that trying to heed this advice sometimes causes tension in the left side and therefore actually hinders the turning action.

A better and more natural way for right-handed golfers to employ a free, strong turning action is to concentrate on the right shoulder. Here's a drill that will teach you the correct motion. Practice it over and over, a few times every day, and you will soon be making a bigger turn that will allow you to hit the ball 10 to 20 yards farther.

Take your normal driver address position. Next, make a backswing, concentrating on coiling your right shoulder in a clockwise direction, up and behind your head. To promote the biggest possible turn, try to get your right shoulder to point directly behind your head when you reach the top of your swing. If done correctly, your left shoulder will be pulled back level and rotated far enough for your shoulder blade to point down at a spot well behind the ball. This drill is of huge benefit, and it really helps golfers who dip to move levelly. It also gets them behind the ball in a power position.

DEVELOPING LAG

If you want power in the swing, the clubhead must lag behind the butt end of the shaft as the forward swing begins.

To rehearse the correct lag position, slowly employ the downswing motion. As you lower the clubshaft, retain the angle you created in the backswing. In other words, hold the same angle you had at the top. Stop when the shaft of the club is pretty much parallel to the target line and just below your waist.

Practicing this drill regularly will help you learn the "late hit" position common to all power hitters. You'll discover it is a lowering action, not an independent pull of the left arm.

SPLIT GRIP

A big fault among club-level golfers is holding on to the club for dear life through the impact zone in an attempt to steer the ball toward the target. Ironically, the ball tends to fly only a short distance and to the right of the target.

To help you learn and internalize a tension-free, powerful releasing action, practice hitting shots by spreading your hands a few inches apart. This split-hand grip will teach you how to release the hands, wrists, and arms correctly in the hitting area. It also allows the student to feel the body and the legs match up with the arms and the club. It's a great synchronization drill.

HARRY COOPER DRILL

If you look at long hitters such as Tiger Woods, Fred Couples, and John Daly, they all obviously have great acceleration through the ball. They rip through the ball and keep on going, unlike many amateurs, who let speed and power leak out of their swing because they slow down at impact and finish with their arms taut and pointing straight up into the air.

To promote added clubhead speed, swing a driver back and through without trying to hit a ball. Simply swing the club back, then through, trying to get your hands to finish directly over your left shoulder as quickly as possible. Get the shaft to hit your shoulder (quickly). Because you have no chance of becoming ball-bound, this drill will encourage you to make a more powerful, professional, tension-free swing. As soon as you believe you have the feel of accelerating the club, hit some balls, concentrating on letting your left elbow fold down immediately after impact. You will notice added power and distance immediately. Allow the clubshaft to hit your shoulder on every finish to diminish any hand tension that may develop as you hit shot after shot. It's a drill I learned teaching side by side with Hall of Fame legend Harry Cooper at Westchester C.C. in New York.

EXTENDING YOURSELF

One thing I have noticed about long hitters that puts them in a league of their own when it comes to generating power is clubhead extension through the ball. Right after impact, the club does not rise straight up into the air, which is a common swing feature among high-handicap players. The clubhead stays low to the ground for about 18 inches. All powerful hitters extend through impact. Extension keeps the clubface on the ball longer, thus adding compression and power to the shot.

Long hitters are able to achieve this power enhancer through the impact zone by extending their arms. No long hitter breaks the arms in toward the body, like so many weak, off-line hitters. Don't you do this either, or else you will shorten your swing arc and lose vital clubhead speed.

This drill, which I use to teach extension at my power schools, was devised by my old friend the former national long driver champion Evan "Big Cat" Williams.

Address a ball teed up about three inches off the ground. Have a friend step in and move the ball about 10 inches forward in your stance. Next, make a full backswing turn, swinging the club to the top. Swing down and through. To reach the ball and hit it very solidly, you will have to extend both arms dramatically.

This drill demands hard practice to perfect, but after a relatively short period of time you'll see a big increase in your driving distance.

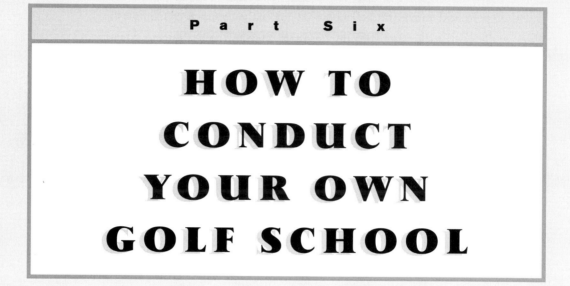

Part Six

HOW TO CONDUCT YOUR OWN GOLF SCHOOL

The beauty of attending your own golf school is that you don't have to limit it to three days or six days. You can—and should—go to school for the rest of your life in golf.

The key to any successful golf school is organization. In our schools we plan our sessions to the minute, devoting blocks of time to each facet of the game, so that by the end of the day and the end of the school our students have received instruction in every aspect of golf.

You should plan your practice sessions the same way. Quality of practice, not quantity, is what counts. Beating five hundred balls until your hands blister wastes valuable practice time. Yes, hitting balls is necessary, but you must understand that practice is a way to learn better technique and movements. Proper positions and motions are best learned by daily repetition. You can learn these positions and motions without hitting balls and often without swinging a club. We have found that spending a few minutes every day on your swing is much more productive than having occasional long practice sessions on the range with nothing in between.

The Rules of Learning

I have three rules that apply to practicing and learning golf:

Rule 1: Golfers learn at different rates. To learn, you have to want to learn. Most of the learning process is up to you.

243

Rule 2: Learn the basics. After you have learned about the proper grip, stance, and alignment, you learn the basic golf stroke in small portions. Do that away from the golf course.

Rule 3: Start in the first grade and work your way through college. If you skip elementary school, you will never reach college. However, by working smart, you can move through the lower grades quite rapidly.

Make a Plan

Your first step in planning your practice is to decide what stage of development you are in with your swing. As I said earlier in this book, if you are a beginner, or nearly so, you might want to concentrate on swinging your arms and hands and letting your body respond. As you become more advanced, you should work on letting the arms and hands respond to the movements of the body. In all cases, the arms and hands and body should work in unison.

Before you go to the range to practice, sit down and write out a plan. First, set your objectives. Analyze your problems and decide on a course of action to correct them. Pick specific drills that will help you with your problems, or with what you are trying to learn at the moment as you become more proficient with your full swing and in other areas of the game. Then figure out how much time you want to devote to each drill on any given day. Be specific! Next, decide how many times a week you want to practice or have time to practice. I'd suggest two or three times a week, in addition to the rounds that you play. But no matter how many times you can get to the range, make each minute count. Finally, decide how long each practice session will last. That depends a lot on your physical condition, strength, and endurance. Keep in mind that too short is always better than too long when it comes to practice. Once fatigue creeps in, your practice ceases to be productive and you can actually learn bad habits.

Once you have determined how long your practice session will be, block out segments. Decide beforehand on the areas of your game that you want to work on and how much time you should spend on each. Then stick to that schedule. Even if things are not going well with whatever you're working on at the moment, don't prolong the allotted time with extra swings. Move on to the next time block on your schedule. Tomorrow is another day, and things will go better.

In every practice session on the range, you should devote time to the following things:

- **Warmup.** Like other sports, golf is an athletic endeavor. You should warm up and stretch properly before practicing or playing.
- **Body drills.** To develop a feel for the overall swing, practice the body drills in this book before you begin other drills or ball-hitting.
- **Specific full-swing drills.** Before you begin hitting balls in normal fashion, do the specific drills that are applicable to what you are working on at the moment. Obviously, these specific drills will change over time. They should reflect specific swing problems that you are trying to correct.
- **Position drills with a club.** These are similar to the body drills, only now you have a club in your hands. Swing from the address position to the top. Then swing back to impact and stop. Then swing on to the finish position. If you want, you can break the swing down into even more positions—halfway back, top, halfway down, impact, halfway through, and finish. In any event, practice going through these positions, so you can develop a

feel for where you are at any stage in your swing. Go through them slowly at first, then gradually speed up.

- **Full-swing ball-hitting.**
- **Specific short-game drills.** These should be related to a particular problem you are having in pitching, chipping, bunker play, or putting.
- **Short-game practice in all four areas.**

How to Make Your Own Video

In modern instruction and at our schools, the days of having a professional lean on a club and point out swing flaws are gone forever. We also are aided by the latest video and computer equipment, which enable us to film your swing and analyze it on the computer.

You may not have the computer capabilities that we have, but you can videotape your swing and analyze it, either on the spot or at home on your VCR. I urge you to do this. What you see yourself doing is often quite different from what you feel you are doing. Seeing a movement can help you make a correction or adaptation more quickly than you can if somebody is telling you what you are doing. You are not dependent on the vocabulary of an instructor. Seeing helps you marry the movement and the feel more quickly. Soon many people will have digitized cameras and will have the capacity to download into any computer. From there it can be sent anywhere for professional analysis. We will begin doing this in the year 2000.

Making your own video is really quite simple. You need to tape your swing from two angles, face-on and down-the-line. For the face-on view—looking directly at the front of the player—position the camera at waist height and directly perpendicular to your target line, so your body will be square to the lens. Allow a big enough frame for your clubhead to be in view throughout the swing.

For the down-the-line view, position the camera behind you, straight down the target line: Camera-Ball-Target all on an extended line. Again, make sure your frame is big enough for the clubhead to be in view as you swing. Here it is crucial that the camera is positioned at least 6 yards behind the ball.

In both cases, make sure the camera angle is exactly as I've described. If it is not, your view of your swing will be distorted. Bad angles will distort what we look for and will cause confusion.

Don't overtape. Just a few swings from each angle will be sufficient. And it's a good idea after each swing to speak to the camera with information on how you felt about that particular swing. Was it a good one? Was it not so good, and if not, why? What mistake did you feel you made? These comments will help when you sit down and view the tape.

Your VCR should have slow motion and the ability to stop an image so it is clear, which will enable you to examine what you are doing at various points in the swing. (But always view your swings at regular speed as well.) If yours doesn't have this capability, getting a new one that does would be a worthwhile investment.

At some point you will want to tape various iron shots, fairway woods, drives, short shots, and even putts. Do this taping periodically so you can monitor your improvement and/or search for a swing problem that's currently bothering you. Be sure to date each set of swings so you will know when they were taken.

Carefully examining these tapes on a regular basis can greatly speed your improvement.

Be Lonely to Be Productive

When you go out to practice, isolate yourself, if that's possible. Pick a spot at the end of the range, away from other golfers, so you can avoid casual conversation and concentrate on what you are doing. You will get much more accomplished in a much shorter time frame. Stick with the elements of the swing you have predetermined for each session.

Use the Easy Clubs

If you are a beginning golfer or if you are working on some serious full-swing changes, I suggest you practice with nonthreatening clubs, like a seven-iron and a five-wood. A seven-iron has loft and is very forgiving. Don't try to learn with a three-iron. That's a club that's intimidating and difficult to hit with, because of its straighter, smaller face. Trying to hit with it will only increase your anxiety. You'll do everything wrong to try to get the ball in the air, and this will slow down, if not destroy, the learning process. The same goes for the driver, which is the longest club in the bag and often brings out the worst in us. Leave it there until you are proficient with the shorter fairway woods. And when you start out, put the ball on a tee for all clubs, including the irons. As you get better at what you are trying to accomplish, you can gradually lower the height of the tee until you eventually put the ball on the ground. You didn't learn to drive a car in a Ferrari on a busy expressway. You learned with your dad in a big vacant parking lot, probably with an older car, going very slowly (at least, I hope you did).

It's the same with golf. You have a training speed at which you should swing, and it has to be relatively slow. You can always add speed as you improve, but you can't learn at full throttle. And you can't learn with different clubs that induce the fear factor. So stick with the nonthreatening clubs and swing them at a rate that allows you to feel what you are trying to accomplish. Usually that's 70 percent or less.

Incidentally, that's not a bad rule to follow for the rest of your golfing life. You will instinctively swing the club fast enough to create adequate clubhead speed. Usually you will instinctively swing it too fast. The problem is to throttle back. Jeff Maggert, a Ryder Cup player, imagines that his driver is a six-iron and swings it at that pace. Fred Couples sometimes practices with a three-wood and tries to swing slow enough to hit it one hundred and fifty yards. This gives you a feeling of togetherness and ease in your swing.

So practice accuracy first, distance second. First make solid contact, then allow yourself to swing harder.

Play golf within yourself. Power golf is only important at the game's highest levels. Even then, the long hitters are still very accurate   if they want to succeed, that is.

Think of an expert pool player. He is always playing for position on his next shot, literally keeping the cue ball in play and in perfect position for his next shot. Rarely will you see a good pool shooter hit the cue ball as hard as he can. It's a good thought for the golfer to keep in mind. And you can't develop this discipline without practicing it.

Set Up a Station

To make your long-game practice productive, you should set up a practice station before doing drills or hitting balls. By simply laying three clubs on the ground, you can check alignment, ball position, and body position. This also makes it much easier to pinpoint swing problems and their solutions. Lay down two clubs, one just outside your ball, pointing directly at your target, and one along your feet, parallel to the first. Now lay a third club just inside your left heel, perpendicular to the others.

As you hit balls, monitor where your ball starts and the direction in which it curves. By knowing that your alignment is correct, you can look elsewhere for your problem.

Some amateurs find laying down clubs every time they practice a little bothersome. I strongly believe it's a bother that pays off, but if this is the case with you, at least lay one club down outside your ball, pointing at the target. You need some indication of how you are lined up. Golf is a game of targets, and you need to know where that target is. Remember, the target line is the most important line in golf.

Practice What You Do on the Course

Practice your routine for all shots, from the full drive to a short putt. Work on that routine on the range so that it becomes . . . well, routine. And practice visualizing your shots. Stand behind the ball and see in your mind's eye where you want the ball to go, even the shape and the trajectory of the shot as it travels there. As we've noted, Jack Nicklaus once said that a successful shot comes from 50 percent visualization, 40 percent setup, and 10 percent swing. But you have to work on that visualization and your routine before it becomes a habit on the course.

Learn to use an intermediate target. Pick a spot a few feet in front of the ball, one you can see just by rotating your head and eyes and that is in line with where you want the ball to start. Then aim your clubface at that spot and align your body accordingly. This is much more efficient than trying to aim the club at the target itself. Again, you have to practice this before it becomes second nature.

While you are practicing, stay focused on what you are working on. Don't jump around from one swing thought to the next. This will create inconsistency and slow your rate of improvement.

Short Game, Short Game, Short Game

In the short-game school, I encourage you to spend at least 50 percent of your time practicing the short game. Actually, I'd like you to spend 90 percent of your golf swing practice time on the short game—not only will you get better around the greens, but as I said, your long game will also improve, because the short swings incorporate the same fundamentals as the long ones. However, I realize this probably isn't realistic. Most amateurs probably spend 90 percent of their practice time on the long game and 10 percent on the short game, and they still can't get on the green in regulation with any regularity due to poor practice habits. And they have decreased their chances of getting the ball up and down because they haven't practiced those short shots enough.

Don't be misled into thinking that the best players hit all good drives and all good second shots. Golf is a game of misses. The best ball-striker on Tour hits about thirteen greens in regulation each round, which means he misses five. If he can't get it up and down, he's going to shoot over par. But he doesn't. He gets it up and down three or four out of five times, makes two or three birdies when he does hit the green, and ends up shooting 70 or under. But he's able to do that because he spends a lot of time practicing his short game.

When was the last time you dumped fifty balls off the edge of the green and practiced your chipping and pitching? Probably never. Well, I'm encouraging you to spend a significant amount of your practice time doing this, along with working on your bunker play and putting. If you don't, you are never going to score as well as you want to—or as well as you can.

Make Practice Fun, Not Work

It's very important that practice of any kind doesn't become drudgery. Have some fun with it. When you are practicing your full swing, pick an object on the range or a tree in the distance (if your range has flags and greens out there, all the better) and practice hitting fades and draws to that target. Work on hitting the ball high and hitting it low. Vary your ball-hitting so it doesn't become monotonous.

Play games during your short-game practice. Conduct your own short-game tests. Take ten balls and see how many you can get up and down from certain distances off the green and with certain clubs. Develop your imagination by looking for different ways to play shots in specific situations. See how many putts you can make from three feet and 10 feet and 20 feet. If you have a friend or friends, set up a competition and go around the putting clock. It's the most realistic way to learn to handle various putts. And if you want to put a dollar or two on the line, that makes the competition even more productive. You'll learn more about how to handle pressure if something is riding on the outcome.

On the Course

If possible, practice on the course. Go out for a while in the evening if it's not crowded and practice playing from different lies and on different slope conditions. Practice your fairway bunker shots. Practice out of rough to see how long grass affects your shots and to determine which clubs you can or can't use under certain circumstances. Play your own scramble, hitting two or three balls each time and playing the best one to get your score. Or play the worst one, a game that really tells you how much bad shots affect your score.

Just remember to replace your divots and repair your ball marks.

Keep a Notebook

Just as our students do in our schools, you should keep a notebook. This is a critical part of your improvement plan. Write down your main swing faults, how you plan to correct them, and how you did correct them. Write down the swing thoughts that work, along with those that don't work. This applies to the short shots and the putts as well as full swings. It's amazing how many times you come across a swing thought that works and you think you'll remember it, but you don't. Two weeks later, it's gone. If you have nothing to refer to, it might be gone forever. As you improve as a player, your concept of the swing will solidify. The concept we teach does not change. But as long as you play, you will undergo changes—your feel will change and your keys will change. If you write down those feels and those keys, you can remember them and, through the use of a drill, recapture them.

A notebook that is well kept is a written record of your progress as well as a plan for your future progress. All the great players with whom I have spent time keep detailed notes. Nick Price has kept unbelievably detailed notes throughout his career. Ken Venturi did the same thing. Jackie Burke, Gardner Dickinson, and Claude Harmon all had detailed notebooks. A number of best-selling books have been compiled from the notes that Harvey Penick kept during his career as a teacher.

Don't depend on your memory. Write it down. And write it down while it's fresh in your mind, after every practice session and after every round, if you found something that helps. Make notes of your playing thoughts—club selection, effect of the wind, how to calculate distance, how to read greens, anything that can affect your score positively or negatively— as well as your practice thoughts. Make sure you know what you write down and what it means. If you go back later and don't understand what something means, get it out of your notebook. And keep referring to your notebook to keep the key thoughts fresh in your mind.

How to Practice at Home

I indicated earlier that brief periods of daily practice are better than an occasional long and tiring session on the range. I realize that most amateurs can't get to the range every day. Work and other activities do interfere with your golf, unfortunately. But the good news is that you can help your golf game a lot simply by doing some things at home.

Think of it as an exercise program. Do body drills in front of your bedroom mirror, or a full-length mirror if you have one, for one to five minutes a day. Check for the correct spine tilt, relaxed shoulders, correct head position, correct shoulder tilt, and correct flex in your knees throughout the drills. Keep a club in your bedroom or your family room and do the same drills with a club over your shoulder. If a golf club is in a convenient place, you must just pick it up.

Home is a good place to work on your pitching swing. Hinge, turn, and hold—you can do it in your family room for ten or one hundred times a day and internalize the feeling of the motion until it becomes mindless, like tying your shoes, an action you no longer have to think about.

Your back yard is a great place to practice chipping and pitching. If you don't want divots in the lawn, put down a piece of carpet or use a tee.

Work on your grip position. Remember our goal—your two hands unify into one hand and your two arms become one giant arm. Monitor your grip pressure. You can go up and down the pressure scale while watching television or chatting with your children. Become sensitive to how tightly or lightly you are holding the club. When driving your car, notice how you grip the steering wheel. How many knuckles are visible on each hand? How much pressure do you exert with your thumbs? You probably should be gripping a golf club the same way you grip the steering wheel.

If your ceiling is high enough (or you can use the back yard), make ten swings in a row varying your grip pressure from one to ten. Maintain constant grip pressure on each swing.

Practice swinging the club to different locations with various grip pressures. Go from address to halfway back with, say, a four grip pressure. Hold for three seconds. Then go to the top, then halfway down, then to impact, then to a full finish, maintaining that four pressure and holding for three seconds at each stop.

Close your eyes occasionally as you swing. With your eyes closed, your feel for the swing movements is enhanced.

Do several repetitions of all these drills five to seven days a week.

If your carpet is smooth enough, home is a great place to practice your putting. Buy a little putting cup or just put down a glass. I'll guarantee you, every pro on Tour is occasionally putting or chipping in his hotel room at night. Lee Trevino once said, "I always get a corner room, because I wake up about three o'clock every morning and I can putt against the wall without bothering the guy next door."

If you can't get to the range as often as you would like, take advantage of home, sweet home. It takes just a few minutes a day, and eventually it will make a huge difference in your play on the course. I guarantee the practice you do at home can and will make a surprisingly major impact on your game.

And speaking of exercise programs, I'd suggest that you do that too. The better your physical condition is, the better your golf will be. You will be able to learn and improve faster, simply because you will have more strength and endurance and will be able to practice longer and more efficiently without fatigue. If you are not on a regimen of strengthening, stretching, and aerobic exercises already, establish one.

Walk whenever possible on the course. This will make you feel better and play better. The game was meant for walking. Golf carts speed you to your ball too fast and it makes your foursome two separate entities. You lose your feel for the course and your timing. You don't allow yourself time to collect yourself properly for the next shot. And you tend to neglect the beauty of the course. It's very sad to see carts overtaking virtually every golf course. I hope you will fight back and always voice your opinion.

One final thought: practice does not make perfect. Perfect practice makes perfect. So any drill you do, any motion you make, do it correctly. Otherwise, you are wasting your time and energy.

I would wish you good luck as you learn more about the golf swing and the game, except that if you incorporate the concepts outlined in this book, you won't need luck. There will be setbacks, because we are all human, but your overall progress will be steady, and you will come to enjoy this great game more and more.

I hope you enjoyed attending our golf school. Stick with the fundamentals that have been outlined and stick with our system. Do that and it's a virtual lock that your game will improve.

ABOUT JIM MCLEAN AND HIS INSTRUCTORS

In 1996, *U.S. News & World Report* rated the Jim McLean Golf Schools the best in the country. This book contains the same philosophies and teaching techniques that earned that accolade for McLean and his Master Instructors.

McLean's accomplishments as a teacher of golf are, as the saying goes, too numerous to mention. He is a PGA Master Professional; owner of the Jim McLean Golf Schools, headquartered at the Doral Resort in Miami; director of instruction for KSL Properties; and director of the famed Jim McLean Golf Academies. He has been a long-time member of the National PGA Teaching Committee, has been a featured speaker at every National PGA Teaching Summit (5), and was cochairman of the 1992 event, and he has attended major teaching summits in Europe, Asia, Australia, and New Zealand. He is an instruction editor for *Golf Digest* and the Golf Channel. He also has a major Internet site: *www.jimmclean.com*. He has written six other books and made five videos and two instructional CD-ROMs.

McLean was the 1994 PGA National Teacher of the Year, 1996 and 1998 PGA South Florida Teacher of the Year, 1986 Metropolitan PGA Teacher of the Year, and winner of the Metropolitan PGA Horton Smith Award in 1987. A college All-American at the University of Houston, he has won more than fifty junior and amateur tournaments and several club professional titles. He has competed in the Masters, where he made the cut, and two U.S. Opens.

But teaching is what McLean does best. He is a passionate student of the swing and the game. His inquiring mind has led him to seek wisdom and counsel from great teachers and great players over the decades. He has learned what works in the swing, what doesn't, and why. And he has developed the ability to teach you how to take the swing onto the course and make it work there.

McLean has been swing instructor to more than one hundred PGA, Senior PGA, and LPGA Tour players, including 1992 U.S. Open champion Tom Kite and Ryder Cupper Brad Faxon. He also coached Cristie Kerr to the number-one ranking in America as a junior and then as the number-one amateur. At this time, Cristie is still the youngest player on the LPGA Tour. But his great love is working with amateurs. He is committed to improving golfers, men and women, at all levels. "Jim McLean is a better teacher than the Dalai Lama," says actor-comedian Bill Murray.

That commitment to better teaching and greater improvement is reflected in the world-class staff McLean has selected and trained at the Doral Learning Center and his other academies. Like McLean, his Master Instructors are all accomplished players and experienced teachers who clearly and concisely deliver an instructional message that is readily understandable. "Without great teachers, you cannot have a great golf school," McLean says.

Among the Master Instructors at the McLean schools are:

Michael Lopuszynski has been with Jim longer than any instructor and has done hundreds of schools with Jim. Captain of his team at Duke University, one of the top hundred teachers in the country as rated by *Golf* magazine, and tutor to many Tour professionals, Mike is an excellent player and has a career low round of 62.

Glen Farnsworth, who has taught and played professionally in

Europe, worked as an assistant to McLean at Sunningdale and Quaker Ridge in New York, was director of teaching at the Maidstone Club on Long Island, and rejoined McLean at Doral in 1991. Glen still works with many top players in addition to performing his school duties as a Lead Instructor.

John Mills, a teammate of McLean's at the University of Houston, where he was a first-team All-American and runner-up in the 1971 NCAA Championship. A head professional in his home state of Maine, Mills was one of the country's top young players. He came to work for McLean in 1993. He is a tremendously intelligent and demanding teacher who gets the job done for his students.

Chris Toulson, who qualified for the PGA Championship at Winged Foot in 1997, was a top junior player, and was a four-year star at the University of Florida. He has won a number of Florida section tournaments and competes at the highest level as a club professional. He has been associated with the McLean schools since 1992. Chris is the director of instruction at Doral, running all Master Instructor training and all Assistant Instructor training.

Marie Mattson-Salter, the head professional at the largest club in Denmark and coach of a strong Danish national team. She returned to the United States to work for McLean and is totally dedicated to teaching. At Doral, she taught Eric Compton, who became the number-one-ranked junior in America in 1998, from age thirteen when he first started playing. Marie is now the director of instruction at Jim's only out-of-country golf academy, Deer Creek in Toronto, Canada.

Shannon Hamel, a fine player at the University of Miami who knows the McLean teaching method inside out. She spent three years training at the schools before moving up to Master Instructor status.

John O'Neill, director of instruction at McLean's PGA West school, a fine player and member of the 1987 NCAA Championship team at Oklahoma State, a head professional in Montana, and for four years one of the top teachers at PGA West before coming to Doral to teach with Jim in 1996. John was the Southern California Teacher of the Year in 1998 and has appeared numerous times on the Golf Channel.

Ben Theobald, a superlong hitter who has played professionally around the world and has a career low score of 61. He is now one of the premier teachers on the McLean staff. Ben works with numerous players on both the PGA Tour and Nike Tour.

Kevin Sprecher played at Arizona State and has been a longtime personal assistant to McLean. He has worked hard at his teaching skills and has been a Master Instructor since 1994. Kevin spends significant time on the PGA Tour working with numerous players.

Steve Sear, the top teaching professional at PGA West before joining the McLean schools. Steve worked as Jim's personal assistant, conducting every private lesson and every school with him. Steve has played in numerous PGA Tour events, played college golf for USC, and continues to play excellent golf. He is now a Master Instructor at PGA West.

Dave Collins, director of instruction at the Marine Links academy in San Francisco, who helped McLean with his famed eight-step swing book and has been valuable in formulating ideas and instruction methods for the schools. He works with the Stanford golf team and many top players in the San Francisco area.

Scott Sackett, who was the director of schools at Doral in 1995 and 1996 and now has the same job at the Legend Trail site in Scottsdale, Arizona. A wonderful teacher, he helped devise the training sessions at Doral. Scott has been the Teacher of the Year in the Southwest and has appeared numerous times on the Golf Channel.

J. D. Cline, director of instruction at a former McLean academy in Seattle, an excellent player and experienced teacher who is teaching now at PGA West. J.D. spent two years working for McLean at Doral. J.D. has been voted Teacher of the Year in the Washington Section.

Carl Welty, director of instruction at La Costa Resort & Spa in Carlsbad, California, for seventeen years. He has worked with some of the game's greatest players, including Greg Norman, Kite, and Tom Watson, and is widely regarded as the world's foremost expert in golf video research. A top-fifty teacher in America and a great friend of McLean's for over thirty years, he now teaches for Jim at PGA West.

Jeff Warne, recognized by *Golf* magazine as one of the country's top hundred instructors. He also is director of instruction at the Atlantic Club in Bridgehampton, New York, and previously was McLean's head teaching professional at Sleepy Hollow, where he worked with many of the metropolitan area's top players and ran an outstanding junior program.

Jerry Mowlds, another top-hundred teacher who spent two years on the PGA Tour. He was the head professional at Columbia Edgewater for seventeen years and is the director of golf at Pumpkin Ridge, site of the 1996 U.S. Amateur and the 1997 U.S. Women's Open. He was the 1984 PGA National Golf Professional of the Year and has won several other national awards.

Karen Palacios, a top amateur player who holds a master's degree in journalism and has written many articles on golf. Fluent in Spanish. She conducts many clinics throughout South America and regularly dispenses advice on the Golf Channel. Karen is in her second year as a Master Instructor at Doral.

Ji Kim, an excellent player who spent two years as a teacher under Craig Harmon at Oak Hill Country Club in Rochester, New York, and three years as a teaching professional at the Precision Golf Learning Center in San Antonio. He was the top instructor at the club in Sonterra, and he has worked extensively under former British Open champion Bill Rogers at San Antonio Country Club. Ji has worked at Doral since 1995.

Margaret Platt-Klaus, an All-American at Auburn University and a top amateur in the metropolitan section. She competed for four years on the LPGA Tour and finished second in a Tour event. She has taken lessons and studied under McLean for sixteen years. Margaret qualified for nine straight U.S. Opens, starting at age seventeen. She is a Master Instructor at Doral.

Jason Jenkins holds a degree in kineology from Penn State and was a member of the Penn State golf team for four years. Jason has helped devise exercise programs and cross-training programs at all Jim McLean Golf Schools and is a Master Instructor.

Dr. Craig Farnsworth has worked for three years at PGA WEST on scoring techniques and visual acuity. Dr. Farnsworth has studied much of the research done by Carl Welty on putting and in teaching putting. Craig has worked with numerous Tour professionals and has designed many special eye improvement techniques.

Jared Isaacs has been the number-one teacher at the famous Northshore Club in Chicago. Jared is a Master Instructor at both LaQuinta Resort and Grand Traverse. He has worked for two years at Doral.

Brian Lebedovitch was an All-American at Loyola University and served as Jim's personal assistant for one season. Brian is currently working with numerous Tour players on both the PGA Tour and Nike Tour.

Debra Spain, a top short-game specialist and one of our top Master Instructors. Debra teaches at PGA WEST and has played in several U.S. Opens.

John Webster, the director of instruction at Grand Traverse, Michigan, for Jim, trained under Dennis Satysher at Caves Valley in Baltimore, Maryland (Satysher was the assistant captain to the 1997 Ryder Cup).

Adam Harrell, Jim's current personal assistant, who has been helpful in writing this book.

Debbie Doniger, a winner of many junior and amateur events, received a four-year scholarship to UNC, where she won the ACC Championship. Debbie later played the European Tour. A former Master Instructor at PGA WEST who currently teaches at Doral, Debbie also instructs at The Round Hall Club in Greenwich, Connecticut, during the summer.

Sandra Palmer, a former U.S. Open Champion and winner of twenty-one LPGA titles. Sandra was a long-time student at the famous Harvey Penick.

Mark Costaregni, in his fourth year at Doral, has won two Colorado PGA Match Play Championships. He graduated from the University of

Florida and played on its nationally ranked golf team. His low competitive round of golf is 64.

Bruce Furman was a teammate of McLean's at the University of Houston. While serving as the Head Golf Professional at the prestigious Hollytree C.C., Furman was named the Head Golf Professional of the Year, Junior Golf Leader, and the Teacher of the Year in the Northern Texas Section of the PGA.

E. J. Pfister is a Master Instructor at McLean's PGA West location. He was a three-time All-American at Oklahoma State University, was a member of the Cowboys' 1987 NCAA Championship team, and won the 1988 NCAA Individual Championship. E. J. played the Nike Tour for three years and the PGA Tour for one year.

The roster of McLean teachers who have moved on—with Jim's recommendation and assistance—is equally impressive. It includes **Mike McGetrick**, now running his own schools in Denver and ranked one of the top one hundred instructors in the country; **Kevin Walker**, also a top-hundred teacher and now a head professional in Nantucket, who has been honored as Teacher of the Year in Colorado and has run his own schools in California; **Charlie Briggs**, now director of golf and general manager at the famous Burning Tree Club outside Washington, D.C.; **Rick Hartman**, now head professional at the prestigious Atlantic Club on Long Island; and **Darrell Kestner**, the head professional at Deepdale on Long Island. Hartman and Kestner are two of the top club professional players in the country.

This cadre of outstanding teachers has helped develop the McLean philosophy and system of instruction, which are passed along to you in this book.